Published by Cicada Books Limited

Edited by Tracey Benton and Ziggy Hanaor
Designed by April
Photography by Ian Tillotson
(www.iantillotson.tumblr.com)
Illustration by Natalie Hill-Cousins
Research by Carrie Maclennan

British Library Cataloguing-in-Publication Data.

A CIP record for this book is available from the
British Library.
ISBN: 978-1-908714-03-9

Cicada Books Limited
48 Burghley Road
London
NW5 1UE

T: +44 207 209 2259
E: ziggy@cicadabooks.co.uk
W: www.cicadabooks.co.uk

Contents

Craftydermy:

A crafty take on taxidermy by Tracey Benton

Taxidermy literally means 'arranged skin'. The Dutch appear to have been the first to attempt to preserve exotic animals after bringing some live birds back from their travels to India in 1518. They were put on public display in a specially heated aviary but some numpty left the furnace on overnight and they all sadly suffocated and died. In an attempt to preserve them, they were skinned, stuffed with Indian spices and wire was used as a kind of armature. Being new to taxidermy, the birds probably looked slightly grotesque but I bet they smelt good.

It was during the 19th Century that taxidermy really began to flourish as a means of preserving wildlife from across the

world to satisfy the Victorian's burgeoning interest in natural history. Unfortunately being a 'sportsman-naturalist' also meant killing shocking numbers of rare wild animals in the name of science. Collectors went to great lengths to secure the 'latest' new species and the sportsmen, in turn, knew that they could command very high prices for the rarest of kills. To put this into context, a rare bufflehead duck fetched £510 in 1853. That's equivalent to over £52,000 today. Taxidermy fell out of favour during most of the 20th Century when the idea of killing for sport lost its charm. Ironically, the move towards conservation and animal welfare was spearheaded by a prominent and rather swashbuckling taxidermist, the American Carl Akeley, who was famed for strangling a leopard with his bare hands. An encounter with a gorilla gave him a change of heart and in the 1920s he declared that killing for sport was abhorrent.

But in recent years, taxidermy has made a surprising comeback. It seems like every trendy boutique or neo-dive bar these days has several mammals gazing down from on high. Presumably these are vintage pieces but it's disconcerting nonetheless. I'm not sure where the trend comes from – perhaps hard times have fuelled a new market in antiques and those tired of the streamlined, clean and clinical urban home want to add a bit of rustic nature and a touch of irony into their living space. Ziggy, this book's publisher, recently worked on a book about the revival of the moustache and wonders if the taxidermy trend could have something to do with a self-aware re-appropriation of traditional views of masculinity. A tongue-in-cheek statement on the concept of man as hunter-gatherer. Whatever the reason, taxidermy is here and it continues to grow apace.

And so too does the craft movement. In a world where lives are increasingly complex and we spend too much time in the alternate reality that is the internet, there has been a massive move towards a greater appreciation of the real, tactile and simple experiences of a long-gone, vaguely remembered past. In a culture with a glut of big brands and cheap mass-produced goods, we appreciate the handmade because we yearn for quality not quantity, the unique rather than the ubiquitous. Craft is no longer associated with knitted-loo roll holders. Craft is cool and it's often a little bit naughty, a little bit irreverent. Wherever there's a new trend emerging, a crafter isn't far behind adding their ironic or cleverly subversive twist. Craft is no longer just craft – for good craft there's most definitely an art to it.

Leopard Hood by Amelia Fever

I own and run a gallery called Atelier, which specialises in crafts from professional British makers. As a maker myself, I have a passion for the contemporary craft scene and wanted a gallery space that celebrated the new wave of beautiful work from talented designer makers both locally (in Devon) and across the UK. I work exclusively with small independent makers and have a great passion for helping to nurture emerging talent; we even have a mentoring scheme, which we run in conjunction with our regional newspaper. I am proud to see so many of Atelier's makers being featured in this book.

I first started to think about the idea of 'craftdermy' when I met Amelia Fever (whose fabulous tiger rug is featured in this book) at New Designers, an annual graduate art show in London. For her final year at university she had created amazing stoles that were a mix of knit, stitch, beading and felting. Her project was making a statement on the fur trade – saying that you can have beautifully crafted garments without killing animals. The work of the contemporary artist Polly Morgan was also on my radar; she was making quite a name for herself in the art world by turning the traditional notion of taxidermy on its head. Using only road kill or animals that have died of natural causes, she puts the specimens in unexpected scenarios and contexts, so that each piece becomes more of a mixed media sculpture than an traditional taxidermy diorama. Then I came across the work of Shauna Richardson who coined the phrase 'crochetdermy' with her astonishingly realistic life-size animal sculptures created using crochet. It all started to amalgamate into an idea... I was excited and inspired and wanted to look at how a variety of craft disciplines could be used for a playful take on Victorian taxidermy.

Still Birth by Polly Morgan

Craftydermy was born. I briefed some of the gallery's makers, and we put together a great exhibition featuring, amongst others, Amelia Fever's animal heads on plinths, Fiona Bates' ceramic ram's head and Emma Cocker's knitted antlers as well as her rather dashing Mr Fox in his traditional hunting gear. The response to Craftydermy was phenomenal – we had a huge amount of media exposure, and fantastic critical feedback – it really blew me away. Here we had the predominantly female crafters responding to the predominantly male environment of hunting and taxidermy in a fresh and irreverent way, and it made even more of a statement than I had originally anticipated.

Meanwhile, Ziggy from Cicada Books had been mulling over the idea of a new book looking at the 'faux taxidermy' phenomena that was emerging on the craft scene and, when she came across the Atelier exhibition, felt that the term 'craftdermy' nailed it on the head. Ziggy had recently published the acclaimed *State of Craft* and wanted to explore this further. We began working together, approaching talented makers to either share their projects or come up with new ones. The response from the crafting community has been thrilling and the projects are fun, tongue-in-cheek and totally capture as well as creatively reinterpret the taxidermy trend. Feel inspired? You should. There's such an awe-inspiring range of projects covering a whole heap of craft disciplines; you can knit, crochet, stitch, glue, stick, sew, stab and fold. There's something for everyone, whether you want to spend a week making or just an hour. It's important to thank the sheer generosity of all the makers featured in this book, as they have shared their work and the often-secret goings on of the making process. Crafters are an awesome bunch and if you've bought this book, you must think so too. Don't be afraid to e-mail your favourite artist and tell them how much you like their project. We hope you enjoy being a craftydermist as much as we enjoyed hunting for these trophies.

Ram's Head by Fiona Bates and *Knitted Antlers* by Emma Cocker

I CAN Make Shoes' BEARFEET SLIPPERS

By Amanda Luisa

Materials

- 2m faux fur
- 1m x 25cm strips of stuffing (no more than 1.5cm thick)
- Scraps of black leather
- Craft foam
- Scissors
- Needle
- Thread
- Sewing machine (optional)
- Craft glue

About Amanda: Amanda Luisa set up I CAN Make Shoes in 2010, and currently runs it with fellow shoemaker Elizabeth Dunn. The I CAN Make Shoes technique is completely unique, and is designed to make the shoe making process as easy as possible, giving even complete beginners the skills to make their own shoes. *www.icanmakeshoes.com.*

What to do

Upper pieces

1. Lay your faux fur on the floor and place your stuffing on top of it. Cut the fur into a strip, approximately 40cm wide and 1m long. Cut the stuffing so that it is 1cm smaller than the fur all around.

2. Fold the fur and stuffing in half lengthways and sew the extra fur down the length of the strip to create a furry tube (fig. A).

3. Place the heel of your foot in middle of the tube (stitching facing the floor), and wrap the tube round so that one side of it crosses over your foot, covering your toes, and the other side crosses over the first (fig B).

4. Holding the crossover in place, remove your foot and stitch down the join. If you are using a sewing machine you will need to really squash the pieces down to get them through.

5. Trim the extra bits at the front and bottom (fig C). You should now have a big round foot.

6. Mark out four toe shapes on the front of the foot using pins. Sew a round toe shape at each pin, and cut away the excess fabric around these shapes.

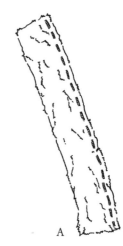

A

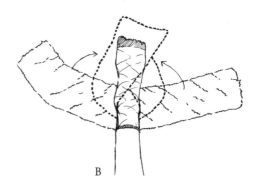

B

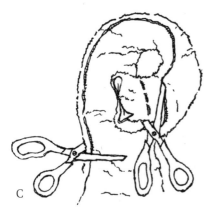

C

Slipper base

1. Place the fur foot upright onto a piece of paper and trace around it.

2. Cut out this sole shape, then draw a paw-print on it and cut that out too (fig D).

3. Trace and cut out two sole patterns onto your faux fur, leaving about 1cm extra around the edges. Remember to flip the pattern upside down for the second trace so that the two pieces match up.

4. Trace and cut out your paw prints on the leather. Glue them to the bottom piece of fur and stitch around them.

5. Place the two bottom pieces of fur together with an oval shape of stuffing in the middle and sew around them with the fur facing outwards (fig E).

6. Place the bottom piece on the floor with the paw prints facing up. Turn the upper piece inside out and place it on top.

7. Now stitch the excess around the top and the bottom pieces together, making sure you get right into the corners of the toes (fig F).

8. Turn the whole thing right way out, so that the paw prints are now on the bottom of the slipper.

D

Claws

1. Trace and cut out 16 claw shapes from the template.

2. Take a thin craft foam and cut out eight smaller claw shapes (approx 5mm smaller all around than your claw shapes).

3. Glue the foam shapes to the back of eight of the claw shapes. Glue a second claw shape on top of that, enclosing the foam on the inside. If you have a strong sewing machine, sew around the claw for added security.

4. Sew the claws into position at the tips of the toes on your slippers (fig G).

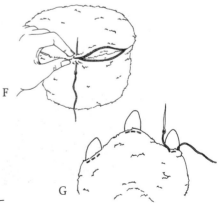

F

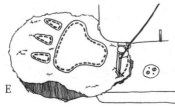

E

G

Hayley Dix's
WIRE BIRD

Materials

- 1.5m of 1.2mm black annealed steel or other wire
- Snipe nose pliers
- Nice looking twig
- Lolly stick
- Epoxy resin glue

About Hayley: Hayley Dix graduated with a first class degree in design and applied arts from Middlesex University in 2011. Since then she has been working on her own projects – finding inspiration in science and the natural world and experimenting with a broad range of materials. *www.hayleydix.com.*

What to do

1. Take your wire and about 10cm in, start by making the foot of the bird. Take the excess and twist it tightly around the leg, just above the foot.

2. Now with the rest of the wire, push out the curve that will be its belly.

3. Carefully trace the rest of the outline of the bird's body, using mostly your hands, bringing the pliers into play only when you have sharp bends, such as the beak or the tip of the wing.

4. When you get to the second leg, repeat the same shape as you did for the first one, and try to get he same length as well. Tightly coil the wire around the second leg – but do not cut!

5. Take the wire across under the belly, and make two tight coils around the top of the first leg. Then pull the wire up inside the bird's body to make the inner detail of the belly.

6. Finish by using your pliers to create a little circle for the eye, and finally cut the wire.

7. You may be able to tweak your little bird's feet so he can stand on his own, or you might want to glue him to a twig. If so, mix your epoxy glue in equal parts, apply a small amount to the feet and twig and hold the two together for a few moments. Then place your bird somewhere safe to dry. Alternatively you can place him on a slice of log, like this one. If so, leave a little bit of wire sticking out at the beginning, when you do the first foot, and drill a small hole into the log. Fill the hole with epoxy and then insert the excess wire into the log so he can stand up.

Merrimaking's
FURRY HOOD

By Meg Tait and Harri Symes

Materials

- 2m faux fur fabric
- Scissors
- Thread
- Tailors' chalk
- Sewing machine
- Button (or other fastening of choice)

About Merrimaking: Best known for their made-to-order animal hoods, Merrimaking have flooded the fields at the summer festivals for the past three years. Their hoods have been worn by Rob Da Bank, Ellie Goulding and Rizzle Kicks. They have more recently moved into limited edition collections. www.merrimaking.co.uk.

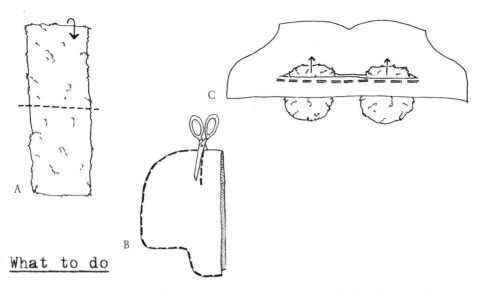

What to do

1. Cut a long rectangle of faux fur, approximately 50cm x 150cm, and fold it in half, fur side up (fig A).

2. Take a hoody that fits you and place it on top of the fur, so that the top of the hoody meets the fold in the fabric.

3. Trace around it, adding 3cm to the front (opening bit) of the hoody, and cut it out.

4. About 7cm in, cut a 8-10cm slit downwards from the top, making sure to cut through both layers evenly (fig B).

5. Now make the ears. Cut four rectangles of fur at 10cm x 12cm each.

6. Place them in two pairs, fur side facing together, and draw semi-circle ears on each pair.

7. Cut out the ears, and sew them together with a sewing machine. Then turn them right way out. Bingo – two furry ears!

8. Open out your hood so that it's completely flat with the fur side facing down. Position the furry ears inside the slit you made earlier, so that flat bit of the ears is wedged in the slit. Now sew up the slit, making sure the seam is on the wrong side of the fabric (fig C).

9. Now fold the hood back in half the wrong way (so fur sides facing) and sew along the curve, starting from the top of the head downwards.

10. Turn the hood right-way out, and attach a fastening to suit – button, lace or Velcro – the choice is yours (fig D).

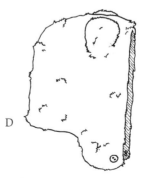

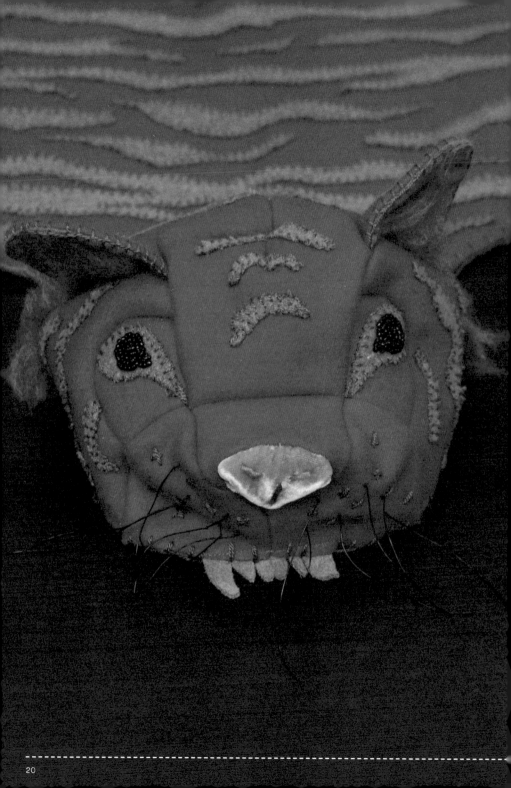

Amelia Fever's
TIGER RUG

Materials
- 1.5m of tiger body fabric
- 2m of contrasting lining/ stripe fabric
- Ball of thin wool
- Black seed beads
- Black jewellery elastic
- 1 scrap of pink velvet
- 1 scrap of non-fraying fabric
- Felt fibres
- Stuffing
- Thread
- Sewing needles
- Sewing machine
- Scissors

About Amelia: Amelia Fever's fascination with taxidermy started whilst studying for her degree in textiles. Her work highlights issues surrounding the fur trade. Using traditional taxidermy shapes, she creates extremely detailed and highly worked pieces, which combine techniques of both hand and machine embroidery as well as laser cut designs appliquéd onto velvets. *www.ameliafever.co.uk.*

What to do

This project is not difficult but involves a lot of hand-stitching so is very time consuming.

The body

1. Choose your fabric colours and textures considering the end use of the piece. This one used thick wool for the body and brushed cotton for the stripes and lining.

2. Pin your body fabric to your lining fabric, draw an outline of your tiger's body and cut it out. Put the lining to one side for later.

3. Cut out some abstract stripe shapes in your lining fabric. If you're using a fabric that might fray, back them with an iron-on interfacing. Then pin them to the back of your tiger and hand-applique them on.

4. Cut out claw shapes and hand-stitch three onto each of your tiger's paws. Choose a thick, non-fraying fabric for this (fig A).

5. Fold a narrow strip of body fabric in half and cut out the tail shape. Sew the two pieces right sides together and then turn right way out. Pin this to the bottom of your tiger, ready to be sewn down later.

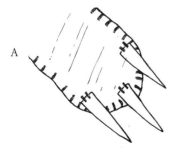

A

The head

1. Turn to the pattern on pp 106-107. Copy the head pattern pieces onto a large sheet of paper and cut them out in your main fabric. Cut out two additional ear pieces in your contrasting fabric.

2. Take your ear pieces in the two fabrics and sew them right sides together, then turn right way round. Hand-applique some stripes onto the back of your tiger's ears, and then blanket stitch around the edges, inserting felt fibres into the side of the ears to give them extra furry texture. Put them to one side.

3. Sew the dart indicated in the pattern into the 'top of head' panel, to create a three-dimensional shape.

4. Sew the eye shapes onto the larger eye panels. Then sew a cluster of black seed beads for the pupil.

5. Sew the completed eye panels to the 'side of face' panels, using notches to match them up correctly.

6. Take your ear pieces and pin them to the 'side of face' panels. Then sew the 'side of face' panels to the 'top of head' panel with the ear pieces wedged in between.

7. Sew the 'bridge of nose' panel to the cheek panels and then sew this to the 'top of head' and 'side of face' panels.

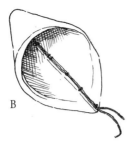

B

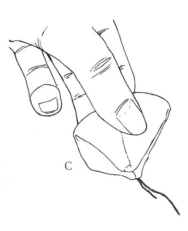

C

8. Cut out the nose pattern from a soft velvety fabric. Take this piece and fold it in half so that the right sides are facing each other. Now sew it into a triangle shape. Turn it right way out and hand-sew the point of the triangle to the bottom of the seam, creating a snout shape (figs B and C). Hand-stitch little dots for detail.

9. Sew your completed nose into the 'bridge of nose' and cheek panels to complete the face shape.

10. Thread black elastic through your tiger's cheeks and knot it both at the front and the back for whiskers. Add extra detail with little cross-stitches on his cheeks (fig D).

11. Applique a few stripes onto the top and sides of your tiger's face.

12. Sew the teeth panel to the back of your tigers jaw. This one used a thick leather to ensure there was no fraying and so that the teeth could be seen from front and back.

13. Cut out two 'back of head' pieces and sew them together. Sew the face to this new piece, adding in some felt fibres on the seam for additional fluffiness. Then hand-stitch a few stripes onto the back of the head. Your head is complete!

Finishing

1. Now go back to your tiger's body. Take the lining piece that you cut out at the beginning and machine sew it to the body fabric, right sides facing with the tail wedged between the two pieces. Leave a gap at the top for the head, and turn right way out.

2. Add stuffing to the head, so it maintains its shape, and attach it to the body by hand, tucking the excess lining fabric inside the structure of the head as you blanket stitch it together.

3. Blanket stitch the outside edge of the tiger for decorative effect.

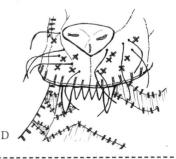

D

Naomi Ryder's
SNAPPY CROC BAG

Materials

- Green wool baize (the fabric that is used for snooker tables - easy to source online)
- Small square of tough fabric in a different green to the baize
- Matching green thread
- Embroidery threads in greens, navy and black
- Bondaweb (transfer adhesive)
- 2 round magnetic clasps
- Sewing machine
- Scissors
- Sharp pencil
- Tailors' chalk
- Large sheet of paper

About Naomi: Naomi Ryder works from her studio at Cockpit Arts in Deptford London, experimenting with illustration in stitch. Her products include cushions, cards, T-shirts, plates and mugs, and she also sells embroidered artwork to commission. She is inspired by the beauty and humour of everyday routines. *www.naomiryder.co.uk.*

What to do

1. Take your sheet of paper, draw a rectangle of 70cm x 25cm, and cut it out, to include a 1.5cm seam allowance.

2. Fold the paper in half, and on one side draw your crocodile-shaped head (fig A).

3. Open the pattern out and pin it to a large piece of baize folded in half. Trace around it with tailor's chalk, and cut your fabric, so that you have two identical pieces. Put one aside for later.

4. Now fold the pattern in half again so that it's rectangular. Pin this onto a second piece of fabric folded in half, and cut it out. This will be the front of your bag (underneath the crocodile's jaw). Again, put one piece aside for later.

5. Cut out shapes for the eyes from fabric of your choice. Bond these onto the face using Bondaweb or transfer adhesive.

6. Look at your magnetic clasps, and then cut two small slits where the nostrils will be, and slot the magnetic clasps into them, pinning them back to secure (fig B).

7. Place the smaller rectangle shape (that you cut out in step 4) on top of the base of your main piece. Fold over the crocodile's head. Make a mark on the rectangle where the magnets/ nostrils touch the fabric. Cut two slits in the rectangle on these marks and insert the other half of the magnetic clasps.

8. Cut two circles of fabric 5mm larger than the magnetic clasps and hand sew them on the back of the small rectangular piece. This will protect the back of the fabric from catching the magnetic clasps.

B

A

35mm
70mm
25mm

C

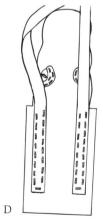

D

9. Cut two more circles of fabric 5mm larger than the magnetic clasps. Bond and stitch these over the magnetic clasps on the face to create a nostril effect. You can embroider as much detailing as you like using backstitch, satin stitch and running stitch.

10. Using more of your second fabric, stitch the croc's eyes using backstitch, satin stitch or running stitch. This one used a plain running stitch after the eyes were bonded and a backstitch to create the pupil (fig C).

11. Cut out a strap roughly 4cm x 90cm. Machine stitch (or hand-stitch securely) onto the back of the larger piece of fabric running from the base up until the point at which the crocodile head folds over (fig D).

12. Now take the duplicate pieces of baize that you put aside earlier, (in steps 3 and 4) and bond the matching pieces together using bondaweb and a very hot iron, cutting out holes for the clasps. This will give your bag structure.

13. Take the smaller rectangle piece and pin it to the croc piece so that the right sides of the fabric are facing each other.

14. Machine sew the rectangle onto the croc piece. Sew three sides, leaving an opening underneath the croc's mouth.

15. Clip the two corners at an angle to reduce bulkiness. Turn right way out to reveal your snappy bag!

The Bellweather's
CROSS-STITCHED STAG

By Claire Brown

Materials

- Wooden laser-cut pendant (available at most craft shops)
- Embroidery threads in colours you like
- Needle
- Scissors
- Felt or fabric to cover the back of pendant (optional)

About Claire: Glasgow-based Claire Brown founded The Bellwether (formerly known as Miso Funky) in 2005, designing and producing cross-stitched homewares with a modern twist as well as kits and patterns. When she's not cross-stitching, she writes about craft and indie businesses, as well as being co-founder of the UK's most popular Kawaii blog, Super Cute Kawaii. She also works as a production manager with a television company. She doesn't get much sleep. *www.thebellwether.co.uk.*

What to do

1. Firstly, find the centre of your pendant. To do this, carefully count the number of squares from the top to bottom and divide by 2. So, if you have 33 squares, for example, the middle square will be number 17. Do the same from left to right and you'll then be able to find the centre square.

2. Cut a length of thread roughly 30cm long and separate it into two strands so it's thin enough to go through the holes.

3. Thread the needle and tie a knot at the end. Traditionally, knots are not used in cross-stitch, but to ensure your design does not unravel, you might want to bend the rules.

4. Locate the centre stitch, take your threaded needle to the underside of the wooden pendant and locate the left hand bottom corner of the square.

5. Draw the thread through the hole slowly, taking care to keep the thread running smoothly so it doesn't get snarled up.

6. Once the thread has been drawn through, insert the needle into the top right hand corner of the same square from the top side of the pendant and pull the thread through gently but firmly (fig A).

7. Now repeat this to form the second leg of the cross – from the under side, insert the needle into the top left hand corner. You can either complete each stitch as you go, or complete a row of bottom legs and then go back and do a row of top legs.

8. When you come to the end of your thread or need to switch colours, complete the cross you're stitching, weave the end of the thread in and out of the back of your stitches a few times and snip it.

9. When you've completed your design, you may want to cover the back of the pendant to hide your working. To do this, cut a circle of felt slightly smaller than the pendant and glue it in place on the back. Alternatively, why not stitch two pendants and glue them together to make a double-sided design? Use your pendant as a necklace, a keyring, a brooch, or switch the colours to red and green for a Christmas tree ornament.

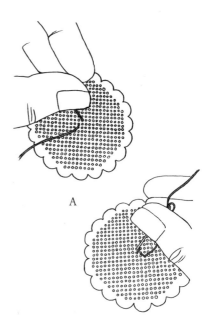

A

Knit and Destroy's FRIENDLY FOX FUR

By Kandy Diamond

Materials
- Pair 4mm needles
- Stitch holder
- 2 balls King Cole Merino blend DK wool in Copper (colour 1)
- 1 ball King Cole Merino blend DK wool in Snow White (colour 2)
- 50cm length black yarn
- Black button
- 10cm of 3mm-wide flat black elastic

About Kandy: Kandy Diamond is the brains and brawn behind Knit and Destroy, making a range of fun, novelty and top-quality knits. When she isn't knitting or roller-skating around, Kandy can be found crafting, drinking tea and co-writing biannual craft zine *Sugar Paper: 20 things to make and do*. Kandy has also been working on more hand knit patterns of her designs... coming soon to a bookshop near you! *www.knitanddestroy.co.uk.*

What to do

This fox is knitted in rib. To make it, start from the bottom and work your way to the top. The finished size is approx 12.5cm (at widest point) by 95cm. Tension: 30 stitches and 28 rows to 10cm over k1, p1 rib using 4mm needles.

The foot

1. Using colour 1, cast on 6 stitches.
   Row 1: (K1, p1) repeat to end.
   Row 2 (increase row): (P1, k1) into first st, *
   p1 k1; rep from * to last stitch, (p1, k1) into
   last st. You will now have 8 stitches.
   Rows 3 - 10: (P1, k1) repeat to end.

2. Slip these foot stitches onto your stitch holder.

The tail

3. Using colour 2, cast on 8 stitches.
   Rows 1 - 2: (K1, p1) repeat to end.
   Row 3 (increase row): (P1, k1) into first st,
   * p1, k1; rep from * to last st, (p1, k1) into
   last st.
   Row 4: (P1, k1) repeat to end.
   Row 5 (increase row): (K1, p1) into first st,
   * k1, p1; rep from * to last st, (k1, p1) into
   last st.
   Row 6: (K1, p1) repeat to end.
   Rows 7 - 18: Repeat rows 3- 6 three more
   times. You will have 24 stitches.

4. Change to colour 1.
   Work 8 rows in k1, p1 rib.
   Row 25 (decrease row): P2tog, * k1, p1; rep
   from * to last 2 sts, k2tog.
   Rows 26 - 27: (P1, k1) repeat to end.
   Row 28 (decrease row): K2tog, *p1, k1; rep
   from * to last 2 sts, p2tog.
   Rows 29 - 30: (K1, p1) repeat to end. Repeat
   rows 25 - 30 three more times, you will
   have 8 stitches.

5. Slip this tail onto the stitch holder along with the foot you've already knitted.

6. Now following the previous instructions, knit another foot.

7. When you have competed this foot, do not break the yarn, and using this yarn, keeping the pattern correct, rib across 8 sts of the foot, cast on 3 sts, rib across 8 sts of the top of the tail, cast on 3sts then rib across 8 sts of the second foot. You will now have 30 stitches on your needle; these 30 stitches make the foundation of the body. Phew, that was tricky, now for a long stretch of straight knitting.

The body

8. Row 1: (P1, k1) repeat across all 30 stitches on needle. Continue working in p1, k1 rib until the body (not including the feet and tail) measures 60cm.

The head

9. Row 1 (increase row): (K1, p1) into first st,
   * k1, p1; rep from * to last st, (k1, p1) into
   last st.
   Rows 2 - 3: (K1, p1) repeat to end.
   Row 4 (increase row): (P1, k1) into first st,
   * p1, k1; rep from * to last st, (p1, k1) into
   last st.
   Rows 5 - 7: (P1, k1) repeat to end
   Row 8 (increase row): (K1, p1) into first st,
   * k1, p1; rep from * to last st, (k1, p1) into
   last st.
   Rows 9 - 10: (K1, p1) to end.
   Row 11 (increase row): (P1, k1) into first st,
   * p1, k1; rep from * to last st, (p1, k1) into
   last st.
   Row 12: (P1, k1) repeat to end. You will now have 38 stitches on your needle.

10. Row 13: (P1, k1) repeat to end.
Row 14 (decrease row): K2tog, * p1, k1;
rep from * to last 2 sts, p2tog.
Row 15 (decrease row): P2tog, * k1, p1;
rep from * to last 2 sts, k2tog.
Repeat rows 14 and 15 until you have
6 stitches.

11. Cast off.

The ears

12. You will be positioning the ears
symmetrically. These will be knitted
straight onto the head of the Fox by
picking up stitches. Start by turning the
head so the nose is towards you and the
right side of the knitting is facing you.

13. Pick up first 2 loops of plain stitch on
outside edge at your chosen position,
then next 2 loops of plain stitch on the
same line, move 1 line up (away from
nose), pick up a further 4 loops in the same
way, move 1 line up, pick up a further 4
loops, you should have picked up 12 loops
in total.

14. Row 1: (K1, p1) repeat across 12 picked up
loops.
Row 2: (K1, p1) repeat to end.
Row 3 (decrease row): P2tog, * k1, p1; rep
from * to last 2 sts, k2tog.
Row 4: (P1, k1) repeat to end.
Row 5 (decrease row): K2tog, * p1, k1; rep
from * to last 2 sts, p2tog.
Row 6: (K1, p1) repeat to end.
Repeat rows 3 - 6 once more. You should
have 4 stitches on the needle.
Then repeat rows 3 and 4 once to take it
down to 2 stitches, cast off.

15. Repeat this process but on the other edge
of the fox's head.

The bottom jaw

16. Cast on 38 stitches in colour 1. Now follow
the instructions for the head, from row
13 onwards to create the same triangular
shaped piece as the head.

Making up

17. Firstly, line up the bottom jaw on the back
of the head; stitch this on passing the yarn
through the back of the stitches only, so
the stitches don't show on the front of the
scarf. Now, stitch the button nose onto the
face, and the black elastic in a loop onto
the bottom jaw. The last finishing touch is
to stitch on the eyes with the black yarn.

Julia Davey's
ENTOMOLOGY LEPIDOPTERA DISPLAY

Materials

- Box frame (at least 3cm deep)
- Mounting card
- An array of vintage paper from magazines or books
- Printed sheet of butterfly images
- White tak or plastic stud earring post stoppers
- Ruler
- Pencil
- Scissors
- Pins
- UHU adhesive
- Pritt stick
- Hammer
- Typewriter (optional)
- Gold pen (optional)

About Julia: Julia Davey is a ceramicist working from a small studio in Bath, making earthenware ceramic items inspired by personal events, places and objects. From illustrated tableware to delicate jewellery, she makes objects intended to be used and contemplated by their owner every day in and around the home. *www.juliadavey.com.*

What to do

1. Remove the back of your frame. If there is a mount inside it already, take it out. If not, cut a piece of craft card the exact size as the back of your frame.

2. Find a butterfly identification sheet either from a book or online. Print it out and then photocopy and enlarge it so that the butterflies are the size you want them to be for your display.

3. Place a photocopied butterfly image on your vintage paper and cut around it carefully (fig A). Do this for as many butterflies you think you might want in your display.

4. Gently manipulate each butterfly to give it a bit of life; roll the edges slightly, and carefully bend them in the middle. You can add detail by highlighting the edges of their wings with a gold pen.

5. Now you're ready to fix the butterflies into the frame. Start by positioning them roughly. Try different arrangements; triangles and lines are very effective. Then use the ruler to measure even spaces between them, and delicately mark the positions with a pencil.

6. Take your first butterfly, and hammer a pin through its body into the mounting board at the mark. Then carefully withdraw the pin. Some of the pins will bend – don't worry – just take another one.

A

7. Take the pin out of the butterfly and put it back in the hole in the board, wiggling it around a little to make the hole slightly wider and easier to find.

8. Now take the pin and put it back in the hole you've made in the butterfly. Push the butterfly about 2/3 of the way up the pin and secure it in place with white tak or earring stoppers. If you are using white tak, wrap it around the pin, just beneath the butterfly. If you are using plastic earring stoppers, put a tiny dab of UHU glue onto the bottom of the butterfly to prevent the stopper from swivelling.

9. Dab the end of the pin into the UHU glue, and then push it into the hole you created on the mounting board earlier. Use a hammer to secure it properly.

10. Repeat for the rest of the butterflies.

11. Allow the glue to dry. It takes a little time, so in the meantime you can twist your butterflies into the best position.

12. Add a typewritten or handwritten label underneath each butterfly to denote its name, date and place of capture.

13. Fit the mount back into the frame, stand back and admire.

Angharad Jefferson's
SQUIRREL CUSHION

Materials
- 1 square of plain fabric
- 1 square of patterned fabric
- Cushion pad
- Water soluble embroidery stabiliser, such as Soluweb by Vilene
- Fineline permanent marker
- Needle or sewing machine
- Embroidery hoop
- Sewing thread
- Embroidery thread
- Scissors
- Pins
- Sewing thread
- Zip

About Angharad: After studying textile design, Angharad worked in the industry designing fabric for a number of well known brands. In 2012, she decided to go it alone and set up a design studio in Glasgow, where she helps people realise their own ideas with a collection of sewing and embroidery patterns. *www.angharadjefferson.com.*

What to do

The embroidery

1. Decide how large you wish the finished cushion and design to be, and photocopy the template on page 104 to the correct size.

2. Take a soluble embroidery stabiliser, such as Soluweb, pin it to the photocopied design and trace the design onto it using an extra fine permanent marker. Usually this will wash away when you wash off the Soluweb at the end, but do a test first – some markers are oilier than others and don't wash away properly (fig A).

A

3. Unpin the Soluweb and tack it onto your chosen plain fabric. Then mount the fabric into a hoop (fig B).

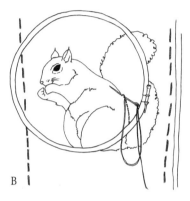

B

4. Now, using colourfast embroidery threads, embroider to your heart's content. This squirrel used a mixture of running stitch, backstitch and chain stitch with black and grey threads. Use stitches which best match the original inky line of your drawing. Look online for some good stitch libraries (fig C).

5. Once you have completed your embroidery, wash away the Soluweb with cool water. Allow your fabric to dry naturally and iron on the reverse.

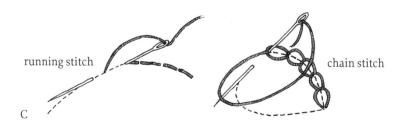

running stitch

chain stitch

C

The cushion

1. Start by cutting your embroidered fabric and patterned backing fabric into two squares. This one measures 50cm per side, but fit yours to the size of your cushion pad. Make sure you cut your fabric 5cm larger than the pad, to leave you a seam allowance.

2. Start with the zip opening. Fold and pin a hem of approx 1cm at the bottom of your embroidered fabric. Stitch it down, fold over again and press. Repeat with the backing fabric. This gives you a nice neat hem in which to insert your zip.

3. Now open your zip and pin each side to your hem. If you position the zip so that the teeth are nestled about 3mm from the folded edge, the zip will then be nicely hidden when it's closed (fig D).

4. Machine or hand-stitch the zip in place.

5. Place the two fabric squares together so that the right sides are facing and pin the remaining three sides of the cushion shut, approx 2cm in from the edge.

6. Sew the three sides together by hand or using a machine. Sew each side individually to make it more secure.

7. Snip the excess fabric at a diagonal from the corners to reduce bulkiness, unless you have chosen a loose weave fabric, in which case you run the risk of unravelling.

8. Turn the cushion right way out, iron carefully and insert your cushion pad.

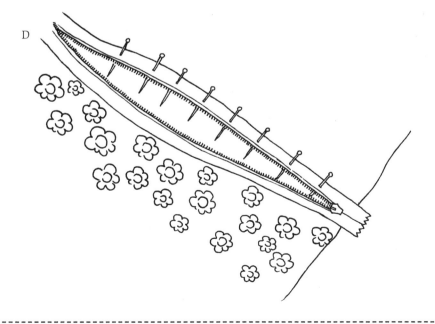

D

Emma Cocker's
CHARLES FOX

Materials

- 50cm x 50cm rust coloured faux fur
- 20cm x 30cm black felt
- 20cm x 20cm beige felt
- Scraps of brown felt
- Sewing thread
- Polyester fibre stuffing
- 2 x black glass head pins
- 5cm x 40cm silk fabric
- Trophy plaque approx 20cm wide x 30cm high
- Circle of wood approx 6cm diameter and 3cm thick
- Needle
- Scissors
- Pins
- Screwdriver and screw

About Emma: Emma Cocker always has a textile project on the go – her great-grandfather was a tailor and her mother is a master of all stitching conundrums, so it runs in her blood. Her range of fabric sculptures and illustrations combine stitching and knitting techniques with reclaimed textiles. Her pieces are nostalgic and humorous, and can be made to commission. *www.emmacocker.co.uk.*

What to do

1. Photocopy and enlarge the templates on p. 105 and cut out (remember to cut two ears and two 'side of head' pieces).

2. Place your fur fabric face down on a flat surface. Pin the head templates onto the fabric so that the pile of the fur is running from the nose end of the fox to the back of the head (fig A).

3. Draw around the templates with a biro, allowing a 1cm seam allowance, and cut out.

4. Join the two 'side of head' pieces wrong way out (fur sides facing each other) and sew from point A to B using either a backstitch, by hand, or a small straight stitch on a machine.

5. Take the 'top of head' piece and sew from point A to C on both sides of the head.

6. Finally join the two side pieces down the back of the head and neck.

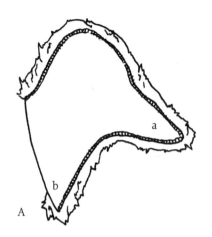

A

7. Turn the head right side out and stuff.

8. Trim the fur on the nose of your fox, so that it is much shorter.

9. Cut two ear templates from the beige felt and from the fur, and pin them together, making sure the pile runs down from the top of the ear to the bottom (fig B).

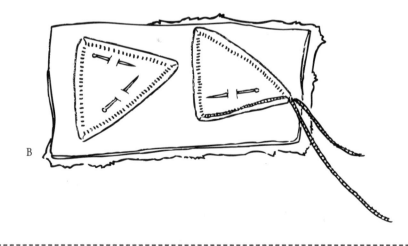

B

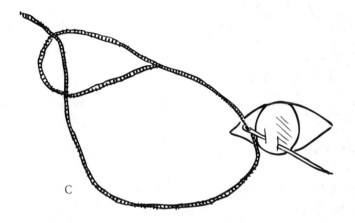

C

10. Using running stitch or a sewing machine, stitch down both sides of the ear, leaving the bottom open.

11. Turn out the ear and over-sew the bottom edge by hand.

12. Then pinch the two bottom corners of the ear together and hand-stitch them at the join.

13. With your forefinger inside the ear, stitch each ear in place on the head using the side seam as a guide – this should run through the middle of the ear.

14. Cut out the nose template and stitch in place, using the black thread. Use the same thread to stitch in the mouth.

15. Cut out the eye templates and stitch the brown felt circle to the middle of the larger black piece with a running stitch (fig C).

16. Using a black glass head pin for the pupil, attach the eye to the head in the appropriate place.

17. Take your circular wooden block and drill a hole in the middle of it. Then place it inside your fox's neck.

18. Cut a circle of felt in any colour – 6cm in diameter. Place this over the wood block and hand-stitch it to the fur, ensuring you can still access the hole in the wooden block. Then screw it to the plaque.

19. If you want to dress your fox in a sharp cravat, fold the strip of silk in half, wrong-side out, sew in a straight stitch, turn it right side out and oversew the two ends.

Caroline Brown's
NEEDLE-FELTED BEAR HEAD BROOCH

Materials
- Merino wool tops (natural white or brown)
- Needle-felting needle
- Protective foam pad/sponge
- Small needle
- Black cotton thread
- Light brown cotton thread
- Small scissors
- Brooch bar/pin
- Strong glue

About Caroline: Caroline creates quirky, personality-filled animal sculptures and accessories using needle-felting, translating her characterful line drawings into tactile three-dimensional objects. She uses areas of painted ceramics and hand embroidery to bring her creatures to life and is particularly inspired by the postures and personalites of bears. *www.caroline-brown-textiles.blogspot.com.*

What to do

Needle-felting works by continuously stabbing wool with a specially designed barbed needle, locking the fibres together and creating felt. The barbed needle is extremely sharp, so felting should always be carried out on a protective foam pad to avoid contact with your hand or other surfaces.

1. Tease out a strand of wool around 15cm in length, 1cm in thickness. The size of your bear head will depend on the size of this piece so make the wool a little thicker if you would like a bigger bear head.

2. Take your piece of protective foam or wadding to work on. Gather the strand of wool and roll it into a ball, starting from one end and folding in the sides as you go. When it is rolled into a tight, rounded oblong shape, flatten down the loose fibres

3. Take your special needle and start stabbing at the wool. To avoid breaking the needle, use a gentle, straight up-and-down motion (fig A). The wool will begin to get smaller and thicker. Hold and pinch in the shape, needling evenly across the surface. Continue this technique until you have a ball that will hold its own shape.

4. Before your wool ball gets too firm, begin to form a nose by pinching one side of the ball and holding this in place whilst you needle around it. Focus your stabbing around the nose, flattening around it and making it into a point.

5. Once you are happy with the firmness and shape of your head you can begin to felt the ears. Tease out a small, very thin strand of wool, around 10cm in length. Twist slightly at one end and begin to roll and gather in, until around 2cm of wool strands are left loose at the end. Hold this roll of wool tightly and very carefully felt into a rounded ear shape, leaving the end loose.

B

A

C

6. Hold the ear onto the head to check the scale. When you are happy with the size and shape then hold the ear on and begin to needle the loose strands into the back of the head. Working into the base of the ear will join the piece initially – if the strands are too long, trim these with sharp scissors and then needle them to blend in. Do the same again for the second ear (fig B).

7. Now is the time to make any adjustments to your bear head – needle more into any areas to tighten up or adjust the expression.

8. Bring your bear to life by stitching on an expression. Using black cotton, start by threading up from the base of the head and use small stitches to create eyes, eyebrows and a nose.

9. If you want to make a little hairy bear brooch then take a different colour thread and stitch in and out all over the top and back of the head. Create small loops all over, rather than tight lines of stitch. Once you have covered the head, take small sharp scissors and carefully cut each loose stitch, to create short loose stitches (fig C).

10. Take a small brooch clasp and use either a strong all-purpose glue to attach, or stitch carefully onto back of the head. Alternatively you could thread a piece of yarn/ribbon through the centre of your bear head to create a hanging decoration.

Tracey Benton's
PAPER MACHE ANTLERS

Materials

- Pencil
- Newspapers
- Masking tape
- PVA glue
- Scissors or craft knife
- Kitchen roll tube
- Cardboard box
- Fine sanding paper
- Acrylic or emulsion paint
- Decorative paper
- Varnish/modge podge
- 4-6 small screws approx 2cm
- Epoxy resin
- Small square of felt
- Small scrap of leather
- Large D ring
- Stick on gems (optional)
- Staple gun (optional)

About Tracey: Tracey explored different avenues of creativity until she discovered clay and has never looked back. Her passion for craft drove her to open the Atelier Gallery in North Devon. Celebrating local and British talent, and nurturing emerging makers, Atelier runs exhibitions, workshops and events. Tracey even gets to make stuff for the gallery from time to time! *www.gallery-atelier.co.uk.*

What to do

1. Decide on a general design for the antlers (how many branches, thickness etc). Look on the internet for inspiration and sketch it out.

2. Using your sketch as a guide, make simple armature using newspaper; take a sheet of newspaper, and twist it round until it's tightly scrunched up. Secure the shape by wrapping masking tape around it tightly. Take another piece and attach it to the first with more tape to be a branch for the antlers. Keep going until you have the basic shape that you decided on. Make sure the paper is twisted as tightly as it can be, so it is dense and firm. You will be bulking it up with paper mache, so don't make it too fat (fig A).

3. When working on the branches, you can use rolled up paper pushed into the join to keep the two pieces pointing in different directions. If you want to make a curving shape, tape some wire tightly to the armature to help it keep the shape, making sure it doesn't stick out.

4. Now to start the paper mache process. Mix some PVA glue with water – four parts glue to one part water. Tear (don't cut) your newspaper into random strips roughly 4cm square.

5. Cover your surface with a bin liner, and put your antlers into a large pot or vase to avoid them sticking to your surface.

6. Soak pieces of the torn newspaper in the glue mixture and smooth them onto the armature. Cover all the surfaces with about four layers.

7. Cut a cardboard kitchen roll tube into two small tubes 6-7cm long (if you don't have one, you can make one from card, securing it into a tube shape with tape). As you're paper mache-ing, periodically check that the diameter of the antlers at the base fits into this tube.

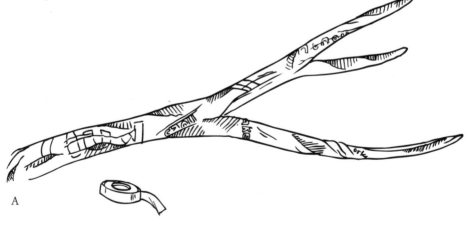

A

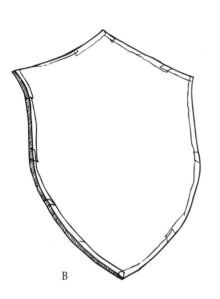

B

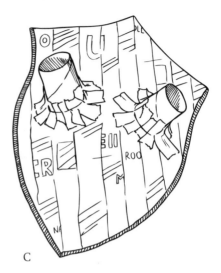

C

8. While your antlers are drying, sketch a plaque for your antlers on the side of the cardboard box. Make sure it's the right proportion by holding it up against your antlers. Cut it out, and then use it as a template to cut out four identical plaque shapes. Tape them together (fig B).

9. Apply four layers of paper mache to the top and sides of the plaque and leave to dry.

10. When your antlers are dry, apply four more layers of paper mache and cover the underside of the plaque. Leave to dry.

11. Keep applying paper mache until you have the size and shape you require and remember to check that the base of the antlers fits snugly into the tubes (fig B).

12. You now need to create an angled fixture so that when your antlers are attached to the plaque they are pointing upwards and out. Mark a point 2.5cm from the base of the cardboard tubes. Draw a rough line from the base up to the mark from the opposite side of the tube. And then another line to the mark around the other side. Fold the card under this line, making small cuts in if you need to. Adjust the card until you are happy.

13. Angle the tubes so the shortest parts of the tubes are facing each other in a 'V' shape, and check the angle of the antlers before you tape the tubes into place with plenty of masking tape (fig C). Then paper mache the outside of the tubes with four layers and leave to dry.

14. Add another four layers of paper mache to the outside of the tubes and leave to dry.

15. Now insert your antlers into the tubes, resting the tips on a pile of books or similar, so that they stay in position. If there is a gap between the antlers' base and the tube, fill it with tightly folded bits of newspaper until it's snug. Paper mache the antlers into place with four layers, so that you no longer see the join between the tubes and the antlers, and leave to dry.

16. Add more layers and leave to dry. Once dry, give it a light sanding to smooth the surface and wipe with a damp cloth to remove any dust.

17. If your antlers are heavy you'll need to secure them in place with screws. Screw two or three screws for each antler from the back of the plaque, making sure each screw is angled to the centre of the antler, rather than the paper mache exterior. Try to get the heads of the screws embedded slightly in the plaque, so they don't affect the hang of the antlers.

18. Now to decorate the piece. This one used a map of North Devon torn up into small pieces but use comic books, vintage magazine or wrapping paper – anything you like. Apply one layer in the same way you did the paper mache and leave to dry.

19. Paint the base – this one used white chalk paint. Apply a little masking tape at the base of the antlers to make sure you get a clean line, and don't get any paint on the decorated surface.

20. If you want to add a little bling, cover the join by gluing tiny gems all over it.

21. Varnish everything using an acrylic varnish or modge podge.

22. Cover the screws at the back by gluing a piece of felt over them.

23. Take your D ring, which you'll use for hanging the antlers, and cut a piece of leather or tough fabric slightly smaller than its width. Glue this fabric about 6-8cm from the top of the plaque using epoxy resin and leave to dry.

24. Put the D ring in place and glue the top part of the fabric over it, leaving a little gap so the D ring can move. For extra security you can staple gun the fabric into place if your piece is very heavy.

Wooden Tree's
FELT WOLF HEADDRESS

By Kirsty Anderson

Materials

- 1m x 20cm of light grey felt
- 1m x 20 cm of dark grey felt
- 1m x 20cm of white felt
- 50cm x 20cm square of black felt
- 20cm elastic
- 30cm x 30 cm cardboard
- UHU or fabric glue
- Stanley knife
- Tape
- Ruler
- Thread
- Needle
- Pins
- Sewing machine (optional)

About Kirsty: Kirsty nests in Edinburgh where she creates plush art pieces using the Scottish woodlands as her inspiration and her granny's linen closet for materials. She likes to recycle as much as she can, making new memories from old ones. Mostly she likes to stitch, rummage in thrift shops and wander the woods. She teaches the odd kids' craft workshop too. *www.awoodentree.com.*

What to do

1. Photocopy and enlarge the template on p.108-109 so that it measures 30cm at its longest point. Cut it out and stick it on your cardboard.

2. Cut out the outline shape. Score then fold the dash lines away from you. Score then fold the dotted lines towards you.

3. Use masking tape to create a three-dimensional shape for the nose in such a way that sides A overlap B (fig A).

4. Cut out two of shape number 2 from the same paper or card.

5. Use tape to secure the gap between points C and D. This will keep the nose propped up, so it doesn't slip out of place. You can use more tape to strengthen if needed.

6. Using a sharp pencil, pierce two holes in E, and put the finished card piece to one side.

7. Take the paper template and cut it in half between F and G so you have a separate nose and forehead.

8. Pin the nose template to the white felt and cut around it, leaving a 50mm allowance so that you can hide the edges of the cardboard.

9. Pin the forehead template to the grey felt and do the same.

10. Using the zigzag templates as a guide, cut strips of felt for the fur (fig B). If you cut down the middle of the felt, you can use both strips. This mask used the following pattern of fur sizes and colours: 1 dark grey, 12cm x 30cm; 2 light grey, 8cm x 30cm; 1 black, 8cm x 30cm; 2 white 8cm x 30cm; 2 light grey 5cm x 30cm long; 3 white 5cm x 30cm long. You can, of course, do it the way that you like, and cut extra strips if you need them.

11. Don't glue or sew anything yet. Lay out all the fur strips on the grey felt forehead so you know what needs to be added or moved around. Start from the back, layering them so that they overlap by 0.5cm (fig C). Start with the darker shades, and move gradually to white (eg. DG, B, LG, DG, W, DG, LG,W, B, LG, W, W, LG, W, W, W). Feel free to experiment with shorter strips in the middle in a different colour.

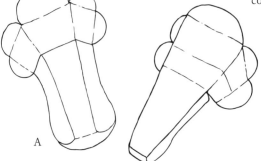

A

C

B

12. Do the same for the nose. Use mostly white for this, with a little bit of light grey dotted in. Remember to start laying out from the back.

13. Cut out the ears from the templates in grey and white felt. Add scrap pieces of felt in the middle for wispy bits. Glue or sew the ears together, then pinch the bottom corners of the ears together and stitch at the join so they prick up a little bit.

14. Place the ears in between the third and fourth row of felt from the back and place them about 9cm apart so they are in line.

15. Now, if you can, take a picture on your phone or camera so you have a reference to work from when you are gluing or sewing. You are ready to MAKE IT HAPPEN. Make yourself a cup of tea first.

16. The best way to keep track of your pattern is to gently flip it over onto a piece of paper and peel off the grey felt backing. Then all the layers are there ready for you to start gluing or sewing.

17. Go through the same process as before but this time glue a thin layer as close to the straight edge of each strip of fur as possible so as not to flatten or glue the jaggy bits. Overlap each bit by 0.5cm. Alternatively, pin each layer and hand-stitch 0.5 cm in – or use the sewing machine to add each layer (fig D).

18. If the felt is hanging over the edge just leave it until the end to fix. If it's too short, add some extra strips.

19. Remember to pin the ears in between the third and fourth row of the layers from the top (don't glue them in yet).

20. Now do the same with the white nose piece; starting at the top, either sew or glue the strips, adding a few extra layers at the top to hide any gaps between the forehead and the nose.

21. Lay the grey felt over the cardboard template, check that the ears are in the right position, and glue or hand-stitch them into place.

22. Measure a piece of elastic that fits your head and tie to the pierced holes.

23. Now glue the grey forehead with its ears attached onto the card frame. It's better if you apply glue to the card first and then stick into place.

24. Do the same with the nose template – sticking or sewing the felt strips on and then gluing it to the card starting from the tip of the nose and slightly overlapping the bottom of the grey forehead piece.

25. Cut out the small black nose and the eyes using the templates and glue them on. If there are any gaps, fill them with extra strips of felt. Put it on your head and howl at the moon (or post pictures of yourself wearing it on the Wooden Tree facebook page)!

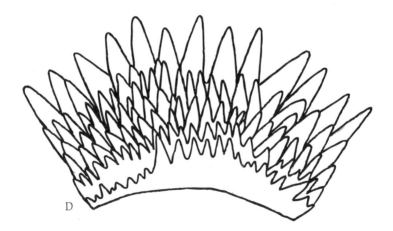

D

In with the Old's
BIRDCAGE LAMPSHADE

By Alice Howard

Materials
- Old wire-framed lampshade
- Newspaper
- Small paintbrush
- Thick tapestry needle
- Pliers or wire cutters
- 2 sheets of pretty wrapping paper
- PVA glue
- Super glue
- Masking tape
- 3 x 10cm lengths of craft wire
- Strips of colourful fabric

About Alice: Alice is the founder of In with the Old, an Islington shop filled with quirky homewares, jewellery and accessories lovingly handmade by Alice and her band of makers. The shop has become a real community hub, hosting craft and photography classes, hair and make-up events and a book club. Get involved through the website. *www.inwiththeoldme.com.*

What to do

The birds

1. Start by making your birds. Three birds are probably enough for a small lampshade, but if you've got a larger one you might want to make more. For each bird, tightly scrunch up newspaper sheets into two pear shapes – one big and one small for the body and the head (the body should be roughly four times the size of the head).

2. Attach the head to the body using masking tape so that the two pear shapes are facing in opposite directions (the peak of the small pear will be the beak, and the peak of the large will be the tail). Wrap the bird with masking tape so it's nice and smooth.

3. Shred a few sheets of newspaper into short lengths of 6cm x 1cm.

4. Mix your PVA glue in a bowl with water – three parts glue to one part water. Dip your strips of newspaper into the mixture and cover the birds with around three layers of paper mache and leave to dry.

5. Take your pretty wrapping paper (or use music sheets or pages from vintage magazines) and add a fourth layer and leave to dry.

6. Paint the birds with a thick layer of glue and leave them to dry.

The lampshade

1. Tear your fabrics into long thin strips – around 1m long and 2cm wide.

2. Take your first strip of fabric and tie it with a knot to a corner point of the wire frame. Wrap the piece of fabric around and around the frame, overlapping each turn slightly to ensure that every bit of wire is covered. When you reach the end of the fabric strip, tie it off and start with a new fabric strip.

3. Paint a layer of PVA glue over the fabric to ensure it stays in place. Pay special attention to the joins between the fabric strips. Trim off the stray ends of fabric and wait for it to dry.

4. Once your birds are dry, make a hole in the base of each of them with your tapestry needle. Take your craft wire and push the end of it into the hole you just made. Then secure the wire with a dab of superglue.

5. When the superglue dries, wrap the remainder of the wire around the frame at your position of choice to secure the bird to the frame.

Clare Nicolson's
FABRIC FLYING DUCKS

Materials
- 1m square of plain fabric
- Scraps of coloured and patterned felt and fabric
- 3 embroidery hoops measuring 21cm, 26cm and 31cm
- Scissors
- Pinking shears/edging scissors
- Needle
- Pins
- Coloured embroidery threads
- Iron
- PVA or fabric glue

About Clare: Textile designer and long time crafter Clare Nicolson has been creating textiles, home accessories and stationery since 2004. She's a collector of all things vintage. Her home is filled with ceramics, textiles and bric-a-brac, which all inspire and often feature in her designs. *www.clarenicolson.com, www.clarenicolsonstylist.com.*

What to do

1. Iron your base fabric to ensure it's crease free. Place it in the embroidery hoops and tighten. Try to make sure there is a good tension on your fabric as this makes it easier when it comes to sewing. Cut the fabric around each hoop, leaving a 5cm gap around the edge (fig A).

B

2. Cut out your small, medium and large duck pieces using the templates on p.112. Pin each template in place and carefully cut out each shape from your chosen felt and fabric.

3. Start with the largest hoop as it will be easiest to work with. Using the finished project as a guide, position the duck in the centre of the hoop, placing each piece in numerical order as per the template (pieces 1-6). Once you are happy with the placement, pin piece 1 in place and move pieces 2-6 to one side.

4. Using two strands of embroidery thread (chosen to compliment your felt/fabric) sew piece 1 into place using a small, neat running stitch (fig B).

5. Pin piece 2 into place and sew using the same method as piece 1. Continue to sew pieces 3-6 into position. Repeat for all three hoops.

6. Once all three hoops have their ducks sewn in, re-tighten your base fabrics and make sure you are happy with the tension and look of each hoop.

7. Using pinking shears, trim the fabric around the edge of each hoop, leaving a 1cm excess. To finish off each hoop, place it duck side down and iron the edges flat. Depending on your base fabric, your edges may need to be secured by glue to stop them from sticking up. You can use a simple PVA or fabric glue, covering the back edge of each hoop with a thin layer and pressing your fabric down until dry to secure.

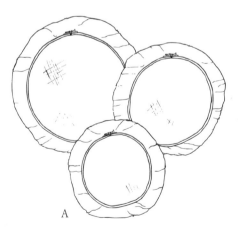

A

Kimberly Diamond's
BIG OL' STAG HEAD

Materials
- Main head fabric
- Antler fabric
- Scissors
- Thread
- 1 pair of toy eyes (or buttons)
- 2 x 45cm wooden doweling rods
- Stuffing
- Shield / plaque (buy these ready made or cut one yourself)
- Fabric glue (such as Gutermann HT2)
- Ribbon
- Needle

About Kimberly: Kimberly is a recent graduate from Visual Communication at the Glasgow School of Art, and still doesn't know what she wants to achieve in life. She started selling her 'guilt free taxidermy' at markets a few years ago, and has recently started dabbling in real taxidermy. *www.kimdiamond.co.uk*

What to do

1. Photocopy and enlarge the templates on pp. 110-111. Pin and cut out the following from your main fabric: 4 ears, 2 main head sides, 1 head strip and 1 back panel. Pin and cut 4 antlers from your second fabric. Make sure to leave a 1cm seam allowance on all pieces. Choose fabrics that are non-stretchy, so that the stag holds his shape and doesn't end up looking a bit droopy.

2. Pin two ear pieces together, right sides facing, and sew them together. Turn them right way out and fold over the bottom edges (fig A). Do a row of stay stitching here (just a quick straight line of stitch to hold the shape – no need to back tack). Repeat for ear 2.

3. Pin two antler pieces together, right sides facing, sew them together and turn right way out. Repeat for antler 2.

4. Insert the eyes to the 'head sides' where marked on the pattern. This one used toy eyes, but black buttons or hand embroidery would do just as well.

5. Sew the ears on to the 'head sides' where marked on the pattern.

6. Now you're ready to start putting Mr Stag together. Pin the long head strip to one 'head side' piece (right sides facing), leaving a space where the antler will slot in. Then pin and sew the other 'head side' piece, leaving a space for antler 2.

7. Now insert the antlers. This is a little bit tricky – the best way to think about it is as though you're inserting a little sleeve into a garment. Pin around the base of the antler and then sew around it, trying to avoid any puckering (fig B).

8. Pin the back panel to the stag face, and sew about halfway down from the top, leaving a nice big hole for your stuffing.

9. Stuff. Don't be stingy with it. Start by stuffing the face, and then do the antlers using the dowling rods. Leave the dowling rods inside to keep the antlers upright. They can be a bit tricky to fill, and you might need a knitting needle to poke the stuffing around the rod into the branches.

10. Hand-stitch the rest of the back panel. Voila! He's looking pretty good now.

11. Glue him to the shield/plaque using fabric glue. Don't use too much – you don't want seepage. Rest something heavy on him overnight, to help him stick to the base.

12. Tie the ribbon around his neck. Use glue to keep the bow in place – stick pins in the ribbon as it dries to keep it from slipping.

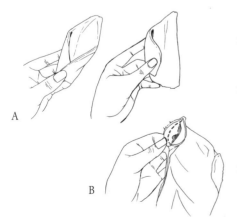

A

B

Louise Harries'
WOVEN HIGHLAND COW

Materials
- Old picture frame or small canvas stretcher
- 25g ball aran weight white cotton thread
- 1 packet of synthetic hair in a ginger colour
- 25g carpet yarn in a natural brown colour
- Toy eyes
- 1 bodkin needle
- Soft wire
- 3mm crochet hook
- Pencil
- Ruler

About Louise: Louise Harries used to work in fashion and is now one half of Prick Your Finger, a rock n' roll haberdashery in east London. This project is a woven portrait of Fergie, Louise's brother's pet cow. He was intended for eating, but the whole family fell in love with him, so he stayed. *www.prickyourfinger.com.*

What to do

1. Take your picture frame and, using a ruler, mark points at 0.5cm intervals along the top and the bottom. Tie the cotton thread at one end and wrap it around the frame front and back, aligning it with these marks. Tie off. This is a simple warp.

2. Thread up your bodkin with a length of the carpet yarn and start to weave it under and over the warp threads. On return, weave over and under so you are beginning to build up a solid fabric-weave. Do this for ten lines. Push the threads down as you go along.

3. Take a length of the synthetic hair and make a Turkish knot. This is a traditional rug knot, which you make as follows: take the hair and double it over. Place the doubled over loop over two warp threads, and then bring the ends under the loop to the front. Go along the warp, making Turkish knots until the end.

4. Repeat these two stages; five to ten rows of plain weave in carpet yarn, followed by a row of Turkish knots with synthetic hair. Keep going until you get to the top of the frame, and make sure you end on rows of carpet yarn.

5. Turn the frame over and cut half way down the warp theads to take the piece off your frame.

6. The warp threads at the bottom of the piece need to be tied together and trimmed into a neat fringe and the warp threads at the top of the piece need to be tied together then split into two, plaited together, then folded over and secured at back to make hanging loops for your piece.

7. Crochet the horns by ch.16, join the begining and end chain to form a magic loop then DC into the loop 15 times, DC in the rnd for 16 rnds or until horn measures 6cm then start decreasing one DC every rnd until you're left with 3 sts or a horn that measures 16cm or so. Repeat for second horn.

8. Take the eyes and push them into a carpet woven strip approx halfway up the piece. Don't worry if they also go through the fur as it gives it a better 3-D depth.

9. Push the soft wire into the horns to hold them in place, then sew the crochet horns on each side and at the top of the piece.

10. Adjust the horns and rearrange the hair, trimming if neccesary. As a final piece of shaping, take two side bits of hair just above the eyes, loop them around and secure under the horns to suggest ears.

Sannapanda's
SHADOW BUNNIES

By Sanna King

Materials

- A small glass or a tealight holder
- Paper
- Black pen
- A4 black card
- Pencil
- Ruler
- Tape measure
- Small sharp scissors or scalpel
- Masking tape or blue tak
- Double-sided tape

About Sanna: Sanna creates a range of screenprinted, handmade accessories in a range called Sannapanda. She takes inspiration from childhood memories of holidays in Finland, and creates her distinctive cut-out illustrations using paper and scalpel rather than a pen or pencil. *www.sannapanda.co.uk*.

What to do

1. You can copy and enlarge the template below, or design your own scenario and draw it out onto a sheet of plain paper. Colour it in with black pen to see if it will work as a silhouette.

2. Measure the height and circumference of the tea light holder. If it's angled (as this one is), measure around its middle.

3. Cut the A4 paper or card in half lengthways. Along the bottom edge of the paper, mark the length of the circumference you just measured, and make two extra marks 5mm from either end. Also mark the height of the tea light holder. Make another mark 15mm from the bottom edge.

4. Draw your design on this strip so that it fits inside the circumference length and so that the top doesn't go beyond the height mark, and the bottom doesn't go beyond the 15mm mark.

5. Taper your design off towards the end, leaving the 5mm sections at either end as tabs.

6. When you are happy with your design, carefully cut it out using small scissors or a scalpel. Keep snipping the excess paper off as you go, so it doesn't get in your way. Make sure not to cut off the tabs at the end.

7. Once you have it all cut out, wrap it into a circle with the tabs overlapping and temporarily secured with a dab of blue tak.

8. Gently position the tea-light holder inside your ring, making adjustments so that it's not too loose or too tight, and marking the final positions of the overlapping tabs. Light a tea-light and check out the shadows that it casts. If it's perfect, use a rubber to gently rub out the pencil marks, and replace the blue tak with small pieces of double sided tape.

9. If there are adjustments to be made to height or shape, retrace the design onto the second half of your black A4 sheet, making these changes. Cut it out again, trying to cut inside the pencil lines, so you don't have to rub them out. Attach a small piece of double sided tape to the end of each tab, and stick them together so that they lie flat.

Antonia Eckersley's
CROCHETED SHEEP

Materials

- 3mm crochet hook
- 2 balls Patons wool blend aran in grey/cream/natural or 2 balls of Rowan Creative worsted wool in natural
- 1 ball of Debbie Bliss Cashmerino Aran in Baby pink (100g) or similar wool
- Small amount of Black wool in similar weight to the Cashmerino
- Embroidery needle
- 2 x 9mm coloured animal eyes
- Small square of polyboard or balsa wood
- Stuffing

About Antonia: After 20 years of working as a graphic designer, Antonia discovered a passion for crochet that has not subsided over the years. Using British breeds wool wherever possible, she has crocheted moose heads, goats heads, dog heads, gnomes and a bust of the Queen. Her quirky creations are rich in personality and detail. *www.crochetfarm.co.uk*

What to do

1. Top of nose

Using cream wool and 3mm hook ch4, ss into first chain to form a ring, ch

Round 1: (RS) dc 6 times into the centre of chain, join with a ss to first st (6sts).

Round 2: (RS) ch (does not count as a st), 2dc.htr into first st, htr.dc into 2nd st, followed by dc.htr into next st, htr.dc into next st, dc.htr into next st, htr. 2dc into last st, join with ss to first dc (14 sts) continue round.

Round 3: ch, 2dc into first st, dc into next st, htr. tr htr into next st, dc into the next 2 sts, 2dc into the next st, htr into the next 2 sts, 2dc into the next st, dc into the next 2 sts, htr. tr htr into the next st, dc into the next st, 2dc into the last st, ss into first dc (22 sts). Continue round.

Round 4: (RS) ch (does not count as a st), dc into the first 4 sts, dc, htr into the next st, htr, dc into the next st, dc into the next 3 sts, htr into the next st, dc into the next 2 sts, htr into the next st, dc into the next 3 sts, dc, htr into the next st, htr, dc into the next, dc into the next 4 sts, ss into first dc (26 sts). Continue round.

Round 5: (RS) Do not chain here, do not dc into base of ss, dc into the following st and into the next 4 sts. Turn.

Round 6: (WS) ch (does not count as a st), dc into the next 11 sts (11sts). Turn.

Round 7: (RS) ch (does not count as a st), dc into the next 5 sts, 2dc into the next st, dc into the next 5 sts (12 sts). Turn.

Round 8 – 9: (WS-RS) ch (does not count as a st), dc into the next 12 sts (12 sts). Turn.

Round 10: (WS) ch (does not count as a st), dc into the next 6 sts, 2dc into the next st, dc into the next 5 sts (13 sts). Turn.

Round 11-12: (RS-WS) ch (does not count as a st), dc into the next 13 sts (13 sts). Turn.

Round 13: (RS) ch (does not count as a st), dc into the next 6 sts, 2dc into the next st, dc into the next 6 sts (14 sts). Turn.

Round 14-15: (WS-RS), ch (does not count as a st) dc into the next 14 sts (14 sts). Turn.

Round 16: (WS) ch (does not count as a st), dc into the next 7 sts, 2dc into the next st, dc into the next 6 sts, (15 sts). Turn.

Round 17-18: (RS-WS) ch (does not count as a st) dc into the next 15 sts (15 sts). Turn.

Round 19: (RS) ch (does not count as a st), dc into the next 7 sts, 2dc into the next st, dc into the next 7 sts (16 sts). Turn.

Round 20: (WS) ch (does not count as a st), dc into the next 16 sts (16 sts). Turn.

Round 21: (RS) ch (does not count as a st), dc into the next 3 sts, 2 dc into the next st, dc into the next 8sts, 2dc into next st, dc into last 3 sts (18 sts). Turn.

Round 22-24: (WS-WS) ch (does not count as a st), dc into the next 18 sts (18 sts). Turn.

Round 25: (RS) ch (does not count as a st), dc into the next 3 sts, 2dc into the next st, dc into the next 10 sts, 2dc into next st, dc into last 3 sts (20 sts). Turn.

Round 26-32: (WS-WS) ch (does not count as a st), dc into the next 20 sts (20 sts). Turn.

Round 33: (RS) ch (does not count as a st) dc into the next 3 st, 2dc into the next st, dc into the next 12 sts, 2dc into next st, dc into last 3 sts (22 sts). Turn.

Round 34-38: (WS-WS) ch (does not count as a st), dc into the next 22 sts (22 sts). Cast off.

To finish: Attach wool to RHS of nose with RS facing, dc along turning edge up to point where crochet changes back to being in the round, this will give you a neat edge for when it comes to joining all the pieces together (roughly 34 sts). Cast off. Repeat the above up LHS with RS facing starting from where it changes from being in the round to rows, attach new wool here and dc up to the top of nose. Cast off. Sew in all loose ends.

into the next 4 sts, dc into the next 4 sts, htr into the next 4 sts, htr-decrease into the next 2 sts, htr into last st (16 sts). Turn.

Round 6: (RS) (crochet into back post of previous sts in this round) ch (does not count as a st) back post dc into back post of first st, bp dc into the remaining 15 sts (16 sts). Turn.

Round 7: (WS) (crochet into the front loops of st in this round), ch (does not count as a st) dc into front loop of first st, dc in front loops of the remaining 15 sts (16 sts). Turn.

Round 8: (RS) ch (does not count as a st), dc into first st, dc into the next 3 sts, htr into the next 2 sts, tr into the next 4 sts, htr into the next 2 sts, dc into the next 4 sts (16 sts). Turn.

Round 9: (WS) ch (does not count as a st), dc into the first 3 st, dc-decrease in the next 2 sts, dc into the next 6 sts, dc-decrease in the next 2 sts, dc into the next 3 sts (14 sts). Turn.

Round 10: (RS) ch (does not count as a st), dc into first 2 sts, htr-decrease into next st, htr into the next 6 sts, htr-decrease into next 2 sts, dc into the remaining 2 sts (12 sts). Turn.

Round 11: (WS) (crochet into back loop in this round), ch (does not count as a st), dc into first 2 sts, htr-decrease into next 2 sts, htr into the next 4 sts, htr-decrease into next st, dc into the remaining 2 sts (10 sts). Turn.

Rounds 12-15: (RS-WS) ch (does not count as a st), dc across all 10 sts (10 sts). Cast off.

To finish: Re-join wool with RS facing at point where chain starts, dc all the way around the three short turning sides to neaten off the edge. (remembering to dc chain dc at corners to give a sharp corner). Cast off. Sew in loose ends.

2. Mouth/chin area

Round 1: (RS) With RS facing, count back 8 sts down RHS of point of nose – the point where the crochet changes from being in the round to going into rows. Attach wool here and dc into the back loop of the next stitch. Continue crocheting into the back loop of this round as follows; dc into the next 6 sts, 2dc into the next st (point of nose) dc into the next 7 sts (16 sts). Turn.

Round 2: (WS) ch, dc into the first st, 2dc into the next st, dc into next 12 sts, 2dc into next st, dc into last st (18 sts). Turn.

Round 3: (RS) 2ch (does not count as a st), htr into first st, htr into the next 5 sts, dc into the next 6 sts, htr in the remaining 6 sts (18 sts). Turn.

Round 4: (WS) 2ch (does not count as a st) htr into 1st st, htr-decrease into next 2 sts, htr

3. Front of chest and under neck

Using cream wool and 4mm hook, make 14ch.
Round 1: (RS) Working in single strand of each
chain, dc into second chain from hook, dc
into each of next 11ch, 3dc into the last
ch (15 st). Working in single strand along
opposite side of ch, 1dc into each of the
remaining 12ch (27 st). Turn.

Round 2: (WS) (crochet into back loop of stitch
all way round) 3ch (counts as a stitch), tr
into second st, tr into the next 7 sts, htr into
the next 3 sts, 2dc into the next st, dc into
the next st, 2dc into the next st, htr into
the next 3 sts, tr into the next 9 sts (29 sts).
Turn.

Round 3: (RS) (crochet into back loops all way
round) 3ch (counts as a st), tr into second
st, tr into the next 9 sts, 2tr into the next
st, tr into the next 2 sts, 2tr into the next st,
tr into the next 2 sts, 2tr into the next st, tr
into the next 11 sts (32 sts). Turn. Round

4: (WS) (crochet into back loops all way
round) ch (does not count as a st), dc into
the first st, dc into the next 12sts, 2dc into
the next st, dc into the next st, 2dc into the
next 2 st, dc into the next st, 2dc into the
next st, dc into the next 13 sts (36 sts). Turn.

Round 5: (RS) (crochet into back loops all way
round) 3ch (counts as a st), tr into second st,
htr into the next 9 sts, 2tr into the next st, tr
into the next st, 2tr into the next st, tr into
the next 2 sts, 2tr into the next st, tr into the
next 2 sts, 2tr into the next st, tr into the
next 2 sts, 2tr into the next st, tr into the
next st, 2tr into the next st, tr into the next
11 sts (42 sts). Turn.

Round 6: (WS) (crochet into back loops all way
round) 2ch (does not count as a st), htr into
firt st, htr into the next 13 sts, 2htr into the
next st, htr into the next 2 sts, 2htr into the
next st, htr into the next st, 2htr into the
next st, htr into the next 2 sts, 2htr into the
next st, htr into the next st, 2htr into the
next st, htr into the next 2 sts, 2htr into
the next st, htr into the next 14 sts (48 sts).
Turn.

Round 7: (RS) (crochet into back loops all way
round) 3ch (counts as a st), tr into second
st, tr into the next 13 sts, 2tr into the next
st, tr into the next 3 sts, 2tr into the next st,
tr into the next 8 sts, 2tr into the next st,
tr into the next 3 sts, 2tr into the next st, tr
into the next 15 sts (52 sts). Turn.

Round 8: (WS) (crochet into back loops all way
round) ch (does not count as a st), dc into
the next 17 sts, htr into the next 2 sts, htr.tr
into the next st, tr into the next 12 sts, tr.htr
into the next st, htr into the next 2 sts, dc
into the next 17 sts (54 sts). Turn.

Round 9: (RS) (crochet into back loops all way
round) 3ch (counts as a st), tr into second st,
tr into the next 21 sts, 2tr into the next st,
tr into the next 6 sts, 2tr into the next st, tr
into the next 23 sts (56 sts). Turn.

Round 10: (WS) (crochet into back loops all way round) ch (does not count as a st), dc into the next 16 sts, htr into the next 6 sts, tr into the next 2 sts, 2tr into the next st, tr into the next 6 sts, 2tr into the next st, tr into the next 2 sts, htr into the next 6 sts, dc into the next 16 sts (58 sts). Turn.

Round 11: (RS) (crochet into back loops all way round) 2ch (does not count as a st), htr into next 19 sts, 2htr into the next st, htr into the next 8 sts, 2htr into the next 2 sts, htr into the next 8 sts, 2htr into the next st, htr into the next 19 sts (62 sts). Turn.

Round 12: (WS) (crochet into back loops all way round) 3ch (counts as a st), tr into second st, tr into the next 23 sts, tr.htr into next st, htr into next 2 sts, dc into the next 6 sts, htr into the next 2 sts, htr.tr into the next st, tr into the next 25 sts. (64 sts). Turn.

Round 13: (RS) (crochet into back loops all way round) ch (does not count as a st), dc into the next 25 sts, htr.dc into the next st, dc into the next 12 sts, dc.htr into the next st (38 sts – it is a short row as you are now going to crochet into the neck). Turn.

Shaping the neck
Round 14: (WS) (crochet into front loops all way round) ch (does not count as a st) dc-decrease, dc into the next 12 sts, dc-decrease into next 2 sts (14 sts). Turn (note: You are turning before the completed round here).

Round 15: (RS) ch (does not count as a st), dc-decrease into 1st 2 sts, dc into the next 4 sts, dc-decrese, dc into the next 4 sts, dc-decrease into last 2 sts (11 sts). Turn.

Round 16: (WS) 2ch (does not count as a st), htr into first st, htr into the next 4 sts, htr-decrease into next 2 sts, htr into the next 4 sts (10 sts). Turn.

Round 17: (RS) 2ch (does not count as a st), htr into first st, htr into the next 3 sts, dc into the next 2 sts, htr into the last 4 sts

(10 sts). Turn.

Round 18: (WS) 1ch (does not count as a st), dc into the first st, dc into the remaining 9 sts (10 sts). Turn.

Round 19: (RS) Repeat as in 18th round. (10 sts) ch (does not count as a st) then continue in dc all the way down right hand edge of work. Rotate 90°.

Fold at base (for neat finish)
Round 1: (RS) ch (does not count as a st) dc again into last st in previous round, continue to the end of row in dc (roughly 40 sts, give or take) ch. Turn.

Round 2: (WS) (dc into back post in this round) ch (does not count as a st), front post dc into first st, (decrease in front post dc, fp dc into the next 5 sts), repeat 5 times, decrease in fp dc, fp dc into next 2 sts (34 sts). Turn.

Round 3: (RS) 2ch, htr all the way to end of row (34 sts). Turn.

Round 4: (WS) ch (does not count as a st) dc all the way to end of row (33 sts). Cast off.

To finish: Neaten off edge in dc up LHS of neck area with RHS facing (8 sts). Sew in all loose ends.

4. Cheek & jaw area (RHS)
Using cream wool and 3mm hook, ch4, ss into first chain to form a ring.

Round 1: (RS) ch, dc 6 times into centre of chain, join with a ss to first st (6 sts).

Round 2: (RS) 3ch (counts as a st) tr.htr into first st (base of 3ch), htrdc into the next st, 2dc into each of the next 2 sts, dchtr into the next st, htr.tr.tr into the next st, ss into 3dr st of chain (14 sts).

Round 3: (RS). 3ch (dc into 2nd and 3rd chain from hook) dc into st at base of 3ch, continue round main ring as follows; (2dc into next st, dc into the next st) x 6 times, 2 dc into the next st, dc into the remaining 2 sts in the 3 chain section. You are back at the beginning (top of teardrop shape) (25 sts). Place a marker here.

Round 4: (RS). (crocheting into back of loop in this round and all the remaining rounds in this cheek section) miss first loop (dc into the first 2 sts, 2dc into the next st) x 3 times, (htr into the next 2 sts, 2htr into the next st) x 2 times, htr into the next 2 sts, 2dc into the next st, dc into the next 2 sts, 2dc into the next st, dc into the last 4 sts (32 sts). Reposition marker here.

Round 5: (RS) 2htr into first st, htr into next st, dc into the next 3 sts, 2dc into the next st, dc into the next 3 sts, 2dc into the next st, (htr into the next 3 sts, 2htr into the next st) x 3 times, htr into the next 3 sts, 2dc into the next st, dc into the next 3 sts, 2dc into the next st, htr into the last 2 sts (40 sts). Reposition marker here.

Round 6: (RS) 2htr into the first st, htr into next st, 2htr into the next st, (dc into the next 4 sts, 2dc into the next st) x 6 times, dc into the next 4 sts, htr into the remaining 3 sts (48 sts). Reposition marker here.

Round 7 (RS) 2htr into the first st, htr into the next 2 sts, (2dc into the next st, dc into the next 5 sts) x 7 times, htr into the last 3 sts (56 sts). Reposition marker here. ✳✳✳

Round 8: (RS) htr into the first 6 sts, 2htr into the next st, dc into the next 6 sts, 2dc into the next st, dc into the next 6 sts, dc.htr into the next st, htr into the next 6 sts, 2htr into the next st, htr into the next 6 sts, htr.tr into the next st, tr into the next st, htr into the next 5 sts, 2htr into the next st, htr into the next 6 sts, 2htr into the next st, htr into the next 7 sts. Reposition marker here and continue crocheting into the back loops of the sts. htr.tr into the next st, tr into the next st, htr into the next 3 sts, trhtrdc into the next st, dc into the next 8 sts, ss into the next st. Turn.

Round 9: (WS). ch (does not count as a st) dc into first st, dc-decrease into next 2 sts, dc into the next 7 sts, dchtr into the next st, htr into the next st, dc into the next 6 sts (18 sts). Turn.

Round 10: (RS) ch (does not count as a st) dc into the first 2 sts, htr into the next 2 sts, tr into the next 4st, tr.tr.tr.tr into the next st, tr into the next 6 sts, tr-decrease into the following 2 sts, tr into the last st (20 sts). Turn.

Round 11: (WS) 3ch (counts as a st), tr into 2nd st, tr into the next 3 sts, htr into the next 5 sts, 2htr.chain.tr.tr into the next st, htr into the next 4 sts, dc into the next 5 sts (24sts). Turn.

Round 12: (RS) ch (does not count as a st), dc into the first 10 sts, htr.chain.htr into the next st, htr into the last 13 sts, (26 sts). Turn.

Round 13: (WS) 2ch, (does not count as a st), htr into the first st, htr-decrease into the next 2 sts, htr into the next 10 sts, 2htr.tr into the next st, 2htr into the next st, htr into the next st, htr-decrease into next 2 sts, htr into next 2 sts, htr-decrease into next 2 sts, htr into next 2 sts, dc into last 2 sts (26 sts). Cast off.

To finish: Where you have the two turning edges, neaten off by attaching wool with right side facing and dc into each st along edge. Cast off and sew in edges.

5. Cheek & jaw area (LHS)

Follow pattern given for RHS of sheep as far as✳✳✳, then continue as follows:

Row 8: (RS) dc.htr into first st, hrt into next 3 sts, tr into the next st, tr.htr into next st, htr into the next 7 sts, 2htr into the next st, htr into the next 6 sts, 2htr into next st, htr into next 5 sts, tr into next st, tr.htr into next st, htr into the next 6 sts, 2htr into next st, htr into next 6 sts, htr.dc into the next st, dc into the next 6 sts, 2dc into the next st, dc into next 6 sts, 2htr into next st, htr into next st, tr.htr ino next st, htr into last 6 sts. Turn.

Row 9: (WS) ch (does not count as a st) dc into first 7 sts, dc.htr into next st, htr into the next 4 sts, tr into next 3 sts, tr-decrease into next 2 sts, tr into next st, tr-decrease into last 2 sts (19 sts). Turn.

Row 10: (RS) 3ch (counts as a st), tr into second st, tr into following 4 sts, htr into next 4 sts, htrtr into next st, trhtr into next st, htr into next 2 sts, dc into next 2 sts, dc-decrease into next 2 sts, dc into last st (20 sts). Turn.

Row 11: (WS) ch (does not count as a st) dc into 1st 3 sts, htr into next 2 sts, tr into next 3 sts, tr.tr.chain.tr.tr into next st, tr into next 8 sts, tr-decrease into next 2 sts, tr into last st (23 sts). Turn.

Row 12: (RS) ch (does not count as a st) dc into first 12 sts, htr.chain.dc into next st, dc into next 6 sts, dc-decrease into the next 2 sts, dc into next 2 sts (24 sts). Turn.

Row 13: (WS) ch (does not count as a st) dc into first st, dc-decrease into next 2 sts, dc into next 6 sts, 2dc into next st, htr.chain.htr into next st, dc into next 13 sts (26 sts). Cast off.

To finish: Where you have the two turning edges, neaten off by attaching wool with right side facing and dc into each st along edge. Cast off and sew in ends.

6. Triangular section of cheek (RHS)

Work into the back loop of st throughout.

Round 1: (RS) with RS facing, attach wool to 4th back loop of st, along from point shown, ss into 2nd st, 2ch, htr into next st, dc into next 6 sts, dc-decrease into next 2 sts. Turn.

Round 2: (WS) ch (does not count as a st), dc-decrease into first 2 sts, dc into next 4 sts, dc-decrease into last 2 sts (6 sts). Turn.

Round 3: (RS) ch (does not count as a st), dc-decrease into 1st 2 sts, dc into next 2 sts, dc-decrese into last 2 sts (4 sts). Turn.

Round 4: (WS) ch (does not count as a st) dc-decrease into 1st 2 sts, dc-decrease into last 2 sts (2 sts). Turn.

Round 5: (RS) ch (does not count as a st) dc-decrease into remaining 2 sts, 2ch (ss into 2nd st from hook), then continue along turning side of work, working in dc to neaten off. Repeat along other turning side in dc to neaten off. Cast off and sew in loose ends.

7. Triangular section of cheek (LHS)

Round 1: (RS) With RS facing, attach wool to 13th back loop of st, along from point shown, ch (does not count as a st), dc-decrease into 1st and 2nd st, dc into next 6 sts, htr into next st. Turn.

Round 2: ch (does not count as a st), dc-decrease into 1st 2 sts, dc into next 4 sts, dc-decrease into last 2 sts (6 sts). Turn.

Round 3: ch (does not count as a st) dc-decrease into first 2 sts, dc into next 2 sts, dc-decrease into last 2 sts (4 sts). Turn.

Round 4: ch (does not count as a st), dc-decrease into 1st 2 sts, dc-decrease into last 2 sts (2 sts). Turn.

Round 5: ch (does not count as a st) dc-decrease into remaining 2 sts, 2ch (ss into 2nd chain from hook), then continue along turning side of work, working in dc to neaten off. Repeat along other turning side in dc to neaten off. Cast off and sew in loose ends.

8. RHS eye

Using cream wool and 3mm hook, chx4, ss into first ch to form a ring.

Round 1: (RS) ch (does not count as a st) dc x 6 into centre of ring (6 sts) ss into first st. Continue round.

Round 2: (RS) 3ch (counts as a st) htr into base of 3ch, 2htr into next st, htr.tr into next st, tr.htr into following st, 2htr into next st, htr.tr into next st. ss into 3rd stof ch (12 st). Continue round.

Round 3: (RS) (crochet into back loop of stitch from here to end) 3ch (counts as a st), tr into base of 3ch, tr.htr into next st, dc into next st, 2dc into next st, dc into next st, htr. tr into next st, 2tr into next st, tr.htr into next st, dc into next st, 2dc into next st, dc into next st, htr.tr into final st, ss into 3rd stitch of chain (20 st). Continue round.

Round 4: (RS) 3ch (counts as a st), tr into base of 3ch, tr.htr into next st, htr into next 3 sts, 2dc into next st, dc into next 3 sts, 2dc into next st, htr into next st, htr.tr into last st, ss into 3rd st in 3chain (30 sts). Continue Round.

Round 5: (RS) 3ch (counts as st), tr into base of 3ch, tr.htr into next st, htr into next 3sts, 2dc into next st, dc into next 4 sts, 2dc into next st, htr into next 3 sts, htr.tr into next st, 2tr into next st, tr.htr into next st, htr into next 3 sts, 2dc into next st, dc into next 4 sts, 2dc into next st, htr into next 3 sts, htr.tr into last st, ss into 3ch (40 sts). *** Continue round.

Round 6: (RS) ss into 2nd st from previous round, ss into next 2 sts, 3ch, tr into next st, htr into next 2 sts, dc into next 11 sts, htr into next 3 sts, tr into last st. Turn.

Round 7: (WS) ch (does not count as a st) dc into 1st 5 sts, ss into next 10 sts, dc into next 4 sts (19 sts). Turn.

Round 8: (RS) 2ch, htr into 1st st, dc into following 18 sts (19 sts) ch, cont round on turning edge working in dc (around 6 sts). Cast off.

9. LHS Eye of sheep

Follow pattern for RHS up to ***. Do not turn – instead continue round as follows:

Row 6: (RS) ss into the next 3 sts, 3ch (counts as a st) tr into 2nd st, htr into next 2 sts, dc into next 9 sts, htr into next 5 sts, tr 3 sts (20 sts). Turn.

Row 7: (WS) No chain ss into 1st 12 sts, dc into next 4 sts, htr into next 4 sts (20 sts). Turn.

Row 8: (RS) 3ch (counts as a st) tr into 2nd st, htr into next 3 sts, htr-decrease into next 2 sts, htr into next 2 sts, dc into next 11 sts (19 sts) ch. Continue round along turning edge working in dc to neaten off (around 6 sts). Cast off.

Finishing the eyes: With right side facing attach wool to turning side of work and dc along edge to neaten off (around 6 sts). Sew in loose ends.

10. Back of head main panel

Using cream wool and 3mm hook, ch 23

Row 1: (RS) dc into 2nd st, continue in dc to end (22 sts). Turn.

Row 2: (WS) ch (does not count as a st) dc into all 22 sts (22 sts). Turn.

Row 3: (RS) 2ch (does not count as a st) htr into 1st st, htr-decrease into next 2 sts, htr into next 16 sts, htr-decrease into next 2 sts, htr into last st (20 sts). Turn.

Row 4: (WS) ch (does not count as a st), dc into first st and following 3 sts, htr into next 12 sts, dc into remaining 4 sts (20 sts). Turn.

Row 5: (RS) ch (does not count as a st), dc into first 2 sts, dc-decrease into next 2 sts, htr into next 12 sts, dc-decrease into next 2 sts, dc into remaining 2 sts (18 sts). Turn.

Row 6: (WS) ch (does not count as a st), dc across all 18 sts (18 sts). Turn.

Row 7: (RS) ch (does not count as a st), dc into first 8 sts, dc-decrease into next 2 sts, dc into last 8 sts (17 sts). Turn.

Rows 8-28:(WS-WS) ch (does not count as a st), dc across all 17 sts (17 sts). Turn.

Row 29: (RS) (crochet into front loop of st) 2ch (does not count as a st) htr into 1st 2 sts, dc into next 13 sts, htr into last 2 sts (17 sts). Turn.

Row 30: (WS) ch (does not count as a st) dc into 1st 8 sts, 2dc into next st, dc into last 8 sts (18 sts). Turn.

Row 31: (RS) ch (does not count as a st), dc across all 18 sts (18 sts). Turn.

Row 32: (WS) 2ch (does not count as a st), htr into 1st 3 sts, dc into next 12 sts, htr into last 3 sts (18 sts). Turn.

Row 33-34: (RS-WS) 2ch (does not count as a st), htr into 1st 4 sts, dc into next 10 sts, htr into remaining 4 sts (14 sts). Turn.

Row 35-36: (WS-RS) ch (does not count as a st,) dc across all 18 sts (18 sts). Turn.

Row 37: (WS) 2ch (does not count as st), htr into first 2 sts, dc into next 14 sts, htr into remaining 2 sts (18 sts). Turn.

Row 38: (RS) ch (does not count as a st), (dc into front posts of sts in this round) fp dc into all 18 sts (18 sts). Turn.

Row 39: (WS) 2ch (does not count as a st), htr into 1st 3 sts, htr-decrese into next 2 sts, htr into next 4 sts, htr-decrease into next 2 sts, htr into next 4 sts, htr-decrease into next 2 sts, htr into last 3 sts (15 sts). Turn.

Row 40: (RS) ch (does not count as a st), dc across all 15 sts (15 sts). Cast off.

To finish: Neaten off turning edges, with RS facing, dc down both sides of work, Cast off. Sew in loose ends.

11. Side of head lower panel (LHS)

Using cream wool and 3mm hook, ch 18

Row 1: (RS) dc into 2nd st from hook, dc into remaining 16 sts (17 sts). Turn.

Row 3-4: (WS-WS) ch (does not count as a st), dc into all 17 sts (17 sts). Turn.

Row 5: (RS) ch (does not count as a st), dc into 1st 7 sts, htr into next 5 sts, tr into remaining 5 st (17 sts). Turn.

Row 6: (WS) 3ch (does count as a st), tr into 2nd st, tr into next 3 sts, htr into next 4 sts, 2dc into next st, dc into last 8 sts (18 sts). Turn.

Row 7: (RS) ch (does not count as a st), dc into 1st 8 sts, htr into next 3 sts, htr.tr into next st, tr into the remaining 6 sts (19 sts). Turn.

Row 8: (WS) 3ch (does count as a st), tr into 2nd st, tr into next 4 sts, htr into next 5 sts, dc into next 6 sts, 2dc into next st, dc into the remaining st (20 sts). Turn.

Row 9: (RS) ch (does not count as a st), dc into first 8 sts, htr into next 6 sts, tr into next 3 sts, 2tr into the next st, tr into the remaining 2 sts (21 sts). Turn.

Row 10: (WS) 2ch (does not count as a st), htr into 1st st, htr into next 9 sts, htr-decrease into the next 2 sts, htr into next 2 sts, dc into the last 7 sts (20 sts). Turn.

Row 11: (RS) ch (does not count as a st), dc into first 10 sts, dc-decrease into next 2 sts, dc into next 4 sts, htr into next 2 sts, tr ito last 2 sts (19 sts). Turn.

Row 12: (WS) 4ch (ss into 2nd st from hook, tr ino base of 4ch), tr into next st, tr.htr into the next st, htr into the next 2 sts, dc into the next 4 sts, dc into last 10 sts (21 sts). Turn.

To finish: For folded edge follow instructions below as in RHS of sheep pattern. Neaten off turning edges, with RS facing, dc down both sides of work. Cast off and sew in loose ends.

12. Side of head (RHS of sheep)

Using cream wool and 3mm hook, ch 18

Row 1: (RS) dc into 2nd st from hook, dc into remaining 16 sts (17 sts). Turn.

Row 3-4: (WS-WS) ch (does not count as a st), dc into all 17 sts (17 sts). Turn.

Row 5: (RS) 3ch (counts as a st) tr into 2nd st, 2tr into next st, tr into next 4 sts, htr into next 5 sts, dc into remaining 5 sts (18 sts). Turn.

Row 6: (WS) ch (does not count as a st), dc into the 1st 8 sts, 2dc into next st, htr into next 4 sts, tr into last 5 sts (19 sts). Turn.

Row 7: (RS) 3ch, (counts as a st), tr into 2nd st, tr into next 5 sts, htr into next 4 sts, dc into last 8 sts (19 sts). Turn.

Row 8: (WS) ch (does not count as a st), dc into 1st 6 sts, 2dc into next st, dc into next st, htr into next 5 sts, tr into remaining 6 sts (20 sts). Turn.

Row 9: (RS) 3ch (counts as a st), tr into 2nd st, tr into next 5 sts, htr into the next 4 sts, dc into the last 9 sts (20 sts). Turn.

Row 10: (WS) 2ch (does not count as a st) htr into first st, htr into next 13 sts, tr into last 6 sts (20 sts). Turn.

Row 11: (RS) 3ch (counts as a st), tr into base of 3ch, htr into next 6 sts, dc into last 13 sts (22 sts). Turn.

Row 12: (WS) ch (does not count as a st), dc into all 21 sts (21 sts). Turn.

Row 13: (RS) 4ch (ss into 2nd st from hook, tr into base of 4ch), tr into next st, tr.htr into next st, htr into next st, dc into next st, ss into next 2 sts. Cast off.

Folded edge at base of both side panels:

Round 1: (RS) Attach wool to bottom RH corner with RS facing and dc into back posts in this round all the way to end (17 sts). Turn.

Round 2: (WS) 2ch (does not count as a st), htr into 1st st, htr-decrease into next 2sts, htr into next 5 sts, htr-decrease into next 2 sts, htr into next 4 sts, htr-decrease into next 2sts, htr into last st (14 sts). Turn.

Round 3: (RS) ch (does not count as a st), dc into all sts in this row (14 sts). Cast off.

To finish: Neaten off turning edges, with RS facing, dc down both sides of work. Cast off and sew in loose ends.

13. Back of head top side panels (same pattern for RHS AND LHS)

Using cream wool and 3mm hook, ch x 10

Row 1: (RS) dc into 2nd st from hook, dc into next 2 sts, htr into next 2 sts, tr into next st, tr-decrease into next 2 sts, leaving 1 st at the end of ch not worked into. (8 sts). Turn.

Row 2: (WS) 2ch (does not count as a st) htr into first st, htr-decrease into next 2 sts, htr into next st, dc into next 2 sts, 2dc into last st (7 sts). Turn.

Row 3: (RS) ch (does not count as a st) dc into all 7 sts (7 sts). Turn.

Row 4: (WS) ch (does not count as a st) dc into 1st 6 sts, 2dc into last st (8 sts). Turn.

Row 5-8: (RS-WS) ch (does not count as a st) dc across all 8 sts, (8 sts). Turn.

Row 9: (RS) ch (does not count as a st) 2dc into 1st st, dc into next 5 sts, dc-decrease into last 2 sts (8 sts). Turn.

Row 10-14: (WS-WS) ch (does not count as a st) dc into all 8 sts (8 sts). Turn.

Row 15: (RS) ch (does not count as a st) dc into 1st 6 sts, dc-decrease into last 2 sts. (7 sts) Turn.

Row 16-17: (WS-RS) ch (does not count as a st), dc into all 7 sts (7 sts). Turn.

Row 18: (WS) ch (does not count as a st), dc-decrease into 1st 2 sts, dc into last 5 sts (6 sts). Turn.

Row 19: (RS) ch (does not count as a st), dc into all 6 sts (6 sts). Turn.

Row 20: (WS) ch (does not count as a st) dc into 1st 4 sts, dc-decrease into last 2 sts. (5 sts). Turn.

Row 21: (RS) ch (does not count as a st) dc into all 5 sts (5 sts). Turn.

Row 22: (WS) ch (does not count as a st) dc into 1st 3 sts, dc-decrease into last 2 sts (4 sts). Turn.

Row 23: (RS) ch (does not count as a st) dc into 1st st, dc-decrease into next 2 sts, dc into remaining st (3 sts). Turn.

Row 24: (WS) ch (does not count as a st) dc into 1st 2 sts, ss into last st (3 sts). Turn.

Row 25: (RS) No chain. dc into 1st st, htr-decrease into last 2 sts (2 sts). Cast off.

To finish: Attach wool with RS facing for LH panel, (WS facing for RS panel) and dc along both turning sides of work to neaten off work. Cast off and sew in loose ends.

14. Ears (2 x cream & 2 x pink) pattern works for both left and right ears

Using cream (or pink) wool and 3mm hook, ch x 27.

Row 1: (RS) tr into 4th st from hook, htr into next st, dc into the next 20 sts, htr into the next st, ending with tr in the last st (24 sts). Turn.

Row 2: (WS) ch (does not count as a st), dc into the 1st 2 sts, decrease, dc into the next 16sts, decrease, dc into the last 2 sts (22 sts). Turn.

Row 3: (RS) ch (does not count as a st), dc into

the 1st 2 sts, decrease, dc into the next 14 sts, decrease, dc into the last 2 sts (20 sts). Turn.

Row 4: (WS) ch (does not count as a st), dc into the 1st 2 sts, decrease, dc into the next 12 sts, decrease, dc into the last 2 sts (18 sts). Turn.

Row 5: (RS) ch (does not count as a st), dc into the 1st 2 sts, [decrease, dc into the next 4 stitches] x2 times, decrease, dc into the last 2 sts (15 sts). Turn.

Rows 6-10: (WS-WS) ch (does not count as a st), dc across all 15sts, (15 sts). Turn.

Row 11: (RS) ch, (does not count as a st), dc into the 1st st, dc into the next 6 sts, dc-decrease into next 2 sts, dc into the last 6 sts (14 sts). Turn.

Row 12-13: (WS-RS) ch (does not count as a st) dc into 1st and remaining 13 sts (14 sts). Turn.

Row 14: (WS) ch (does not count as a st) dc into the 1st st and the next 5 sts, dc- decrease into the next 2 sts, dc into the remaining 6 sts (13 sts). Turn.

Row 15: (RS) ch (does not count as a st) dc into the 1st and the next 4 sts, dc-decrease into next 2 sts, dc into the remaining 6 sts (12 sts). Turn.

Row 16: (WS) ch (does not count as a st) dc into the 1st st, dc-decrease into next 2 sts, dc into the next 2 sts, dc-decrease into next 2 sts, dc into the next 2 sts, dc-decrease into next 2 sts, dc into the last st (9 sts). Turn.

Row 17: (RS) dc (does not count as a st) dc into the 1st st, dc-decrease into next 2 sts, dc into the next 3 sts, dc-decrease into next 2 sts, dc into the last st (7 sts). Turn.

Row 18: (WS) dc (does not count as a st) dc into the 1st st, dc-decrease into next 2 sts, dc into the next st, dc-decrease into next 2 sts, dc into the last st (5 sts). Turn.

Row 19: (RS) dc (does not count as a st) dc-decrease into the 1st 2 sts, dc into the next st, dc-decrease into the last 2 sts (3 sts). Turn.

Row 20: (WS) dc (does not count as a st) dc-decrease into the 1st 2 sts, dc into the last st (2 sts). Turn.

Row 21: (RS) dc (does not count as a st) dc-decrease into remaining 2 sts. Cast off.

To finish: Sandwich a cream ear and a pink ear together. With the pink side facing you, crochet together starting in bottom RH corner. Use dc through both pieces of work ending in the LH corner. Cast off leaving a long enough tail to sew along the bottom edge using over cast sts. Sew in loose ends.

15. Finishing the sheep

Join all the pieces together using woven stitch so that your seams are invisible. In this pattern every edge is finished in dc, so there should be no turning edge seams.

Lay the pieces side by side, right sides facing up, and line up the stitches of the rows.

Thread a yarn needle with the same yarn you used for the piece, and stitch the edges together, bringing the needle up from back to front, through the outer loops on the tops of the stitches.

Once all pieces of the head are attached, finally position ears at right angles on either side of head using over cast stitch.

16. Embroidery for mouth and nose

Thread a tapestry needle with a very long length of wool (it always takes more than you think). Starting at the left hand side of the nose, chain stitch two stitches side by side. Then in the centre of these two stitches, begin chain and chain round to right hand side of the mouth (around 10 chains). Double chain at the end.

Pull yarn back out at the halfway point between completed nose embroidery, embroider 3 chains here and then in the center of the 3 chains, chain embroider 3 chains down to mouth area.

Pull yarn back through work and out at the left hand side of where you will begin chain for mouth area, (a shorter amount of chains looks more effective; around 7chains). Finally sew in loose ends into back of work and cast off.

17. Final touches

Take the toy eyes and push the backs of eyes through the center eye pieces, securing with the fastenings.

Stuff the head with synthetic filling and squidge into shape.

Place the head on a sheet of paper and draw around the base of the neck with a pencil. Cut out the shape, put it on a piece of polyboard or balsa wood and cut around it with a scalpel.

Punch a hole through the polyboard or balsa wood in the centre, around 4cm through the edge.

Templates

Angharad Jefferson's SQUIRREL CUSHION - pp.44-47

The Bellweather's CROSS-STITCHED STAG, by Claire Brown - pp.30-3

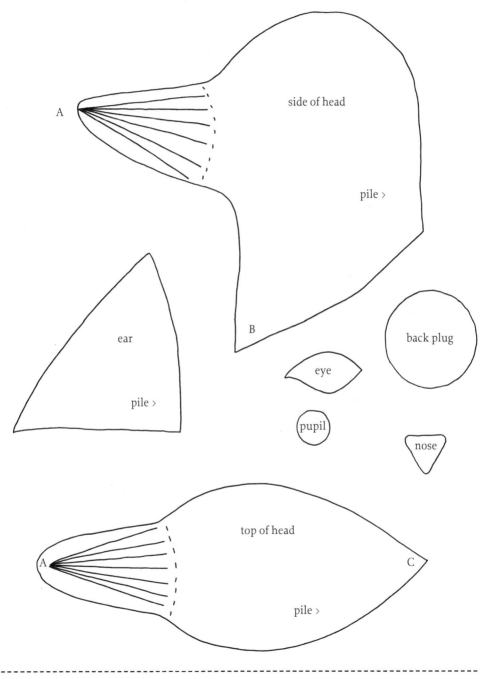

A

side of head

pile ›

ear

pile ›

B

eye

back plug

pupil

nose

A

top of head

C

pile ›

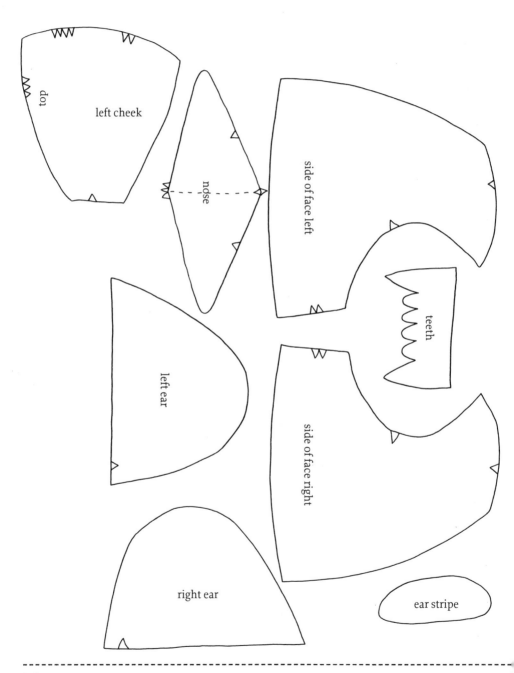

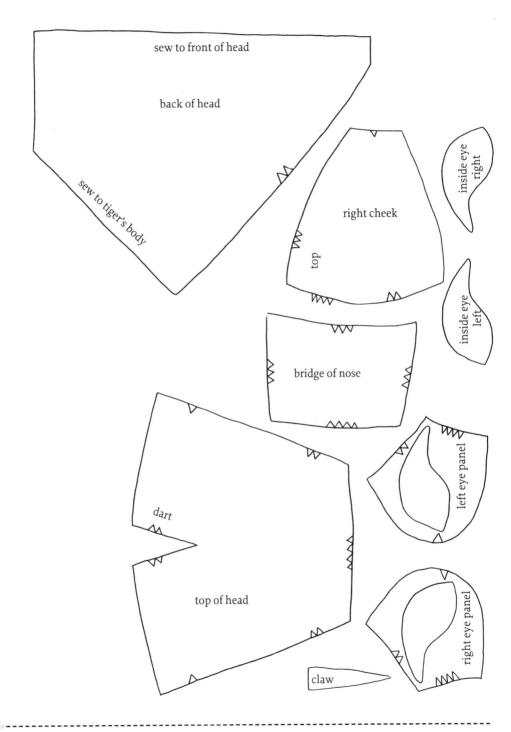

sew to front of head

back of head

sew to tiger's body

right cheek

top

inside eye right

inside eye left

bridge of nose

left eye panel

dart

top of head

right eye panel

claw

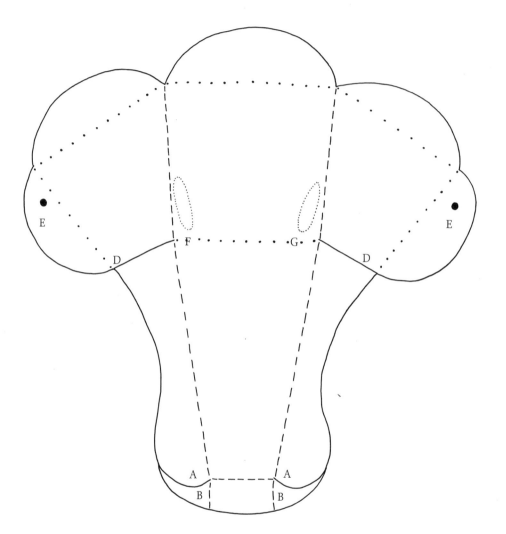

_____ cut

- - - - - - - - - fold away from you

.... fold towards you

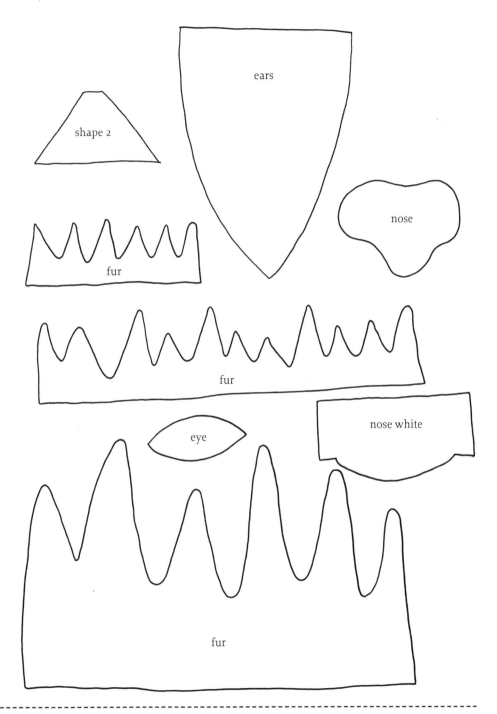

Kimberly Diamond's BIG OL' STAG HEAD - pp.78-81

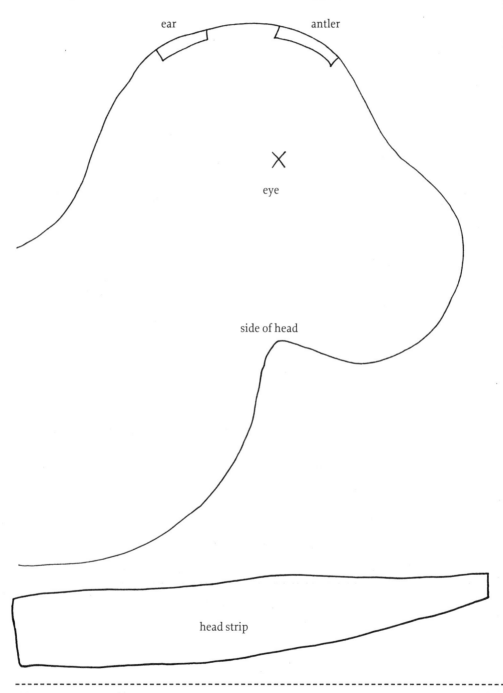

ear

antler

eye

side of head

head strip

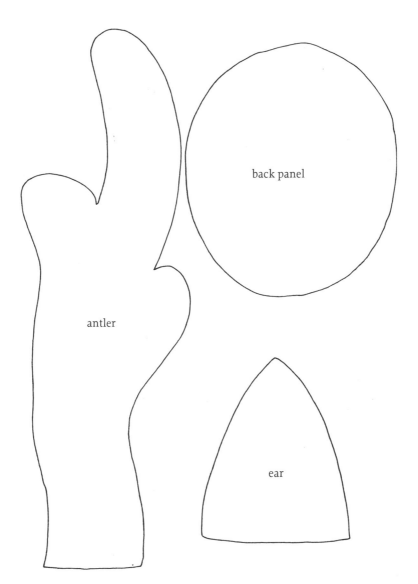

back panel

antler

ear

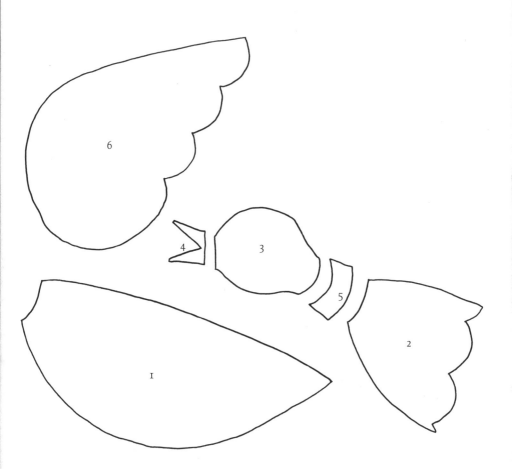